THE ENCYCLOPEDIA OF
Quilting & Patchwork
TECHNIQUES

THE ENCYCLOPEDIA OF
Quilting & Patchwork
TECHNIQUES

Katharine Guerrier

Search Press

A QUARTO BOOK

Published in 2016 by
Search Press Ltd
Wellwood
North Farm Road
Tunbridge Wells
Kent TN2 3DR

ISBN: 978-1-78221-476-2

Conceived, designed and produced by
Quarto Publishing plc
The Old Brewery
6 Blundell Street
London N7 9BH
www.quartoknows.com

QUAR.EQT2

Assistant Editor: Georgia Cherry
Art Director: Caroline Guest
Designer: Julie Francis
Creative Director: Moira Clinch
Publisher: Paul Carslake

Printed in China by 1010 Printing
International Ltd

Credits: page 2: Improvisation 2 by
Katharine Guerrier; page 4: Watermelon
Dreams by Diane Melm (detail); page 5:
Crop Circles by Pat Bishop.

Contents

Introduction

From a craft born of necessity quiltmaking has progressed to a highly decorative art form. The combination of patchwork, appliqué and quilting which together make up this versatile craft affords it great potential as a medium for self-expression.

This recommends it to quiltmakers experimenting on all levels, from simple traditional designs to elaborate investigations of colour and pattern, and with a wide range of motives, from decorating the home, commemorating a special event, raising money for charity or creating a work of art. The materials and equipment required are easily obtainable and relatively cheap – in some cases even recyclable from other sewing projects. Although there are now quilt shops selling a wide range of specialist equipment for the quiltmaker, a beginner needs only the basics to make a start: fabrics, a sewing kit and some tools for drawing and making templates.

MONOCHROME
DEBBIE JESKE
73.5 x 79 cm (29 x 31 in)
This quilt was inspired by
improvisation under the
influence of Krista Hennebury.

Anatomy of the Quilt

The craft of quiltmaking uses a range of technical terms to distinguish different parts of the quilt. Key aspects of this 'anatomy' are illustrated opposite. It is important to remember that the quilt itself is basically a fabric sandwich consisting of three layers: the top (often covered with decorative patchwork or appliqué), the filler and the backing. The sandwich is held together by the quilting, which is often also an important decorative feature. The binding finishes the edges of the quilt to neaten and enclose the raw edges and filler.

It is worth pointing out the technical distinction between patchwork and appliqué. Patchwork, also known as piecing, is the technique of sewing small pieces of fabric together to create a large piece. Appliqué is the technique of cutting out fabric pieces and stitching them to a background, usually to create a pictorial or representational design.

A quilt in progress, showing the Morning Star design. A freestanding quilting frame helps to keep the quilt taut over the area that is being worked.

SASHING OR LATTICE STRIPS
A grid of fabric strips which can be used to separate out and to frame the blocks.

BLOCKS
The design unit made from either patchwork or appliqué, or a combination of the two, repeated to make the quilt top. These can be set straight or 'on point', that is diagonally so they form a diamond shape.

QUILT TOP
The top layer of the quilt, which can be patchwork, appliqué or wholecloth.

WADDING OR BATTING
The warm interlining or filler forming the inner layer of the quilt.

BACKING
The fabric on the back of the quilt.

QUILTING
Stitching, often decorative, which holds the three layers of the quilt together.

BORDER
A frame surrounding the main part of the quilt. It can be plain or patchwork.

Equipment

You will probably already have many of the things necessary for making a start in patchwork and quilting. Have a look through your general sewing equipment before deciding what else you need. It is wise to buy the best quality tools and materials that you can afford, and if you are in doubt about making a choice when choosing an expensive item like a new sewing machine, ask the advice of someone with experience, rather than being persuaded by an enthusiastic salesperson. Patchwork was originally a craft of necessity and although today there is a whole industry devoted to supplying the needs of quilters, you can make a start with the basics and add to these as you progress, by which time you will have more idea of what will be useful and which products are just gimmicks.

The basic list of equipment for cutting and sewing should contain the following:

1 A top quality pair of dressmaking scissors, a pair of paper scissors and a pair of fine embroidery scissors for trimming threads and seam allowances.

2 Glass-headed and wedding dress pins to cater for different thicknesses of fabric.

3 Hand sewing needles, sharps no. 8 or 9 for general sewing and betweens no. 8 or 9 for quilting. The shorter needles have higher numbers.

4 Threads: a variety of colours for machine and hand sewing. A thicker thread is available for hand quilting.

5 Thimble: essential for hand quilting and if you intend to hand stitch patchwork. There are various designs of thimble especially for quilting, some metal with a flattened top, some plastic or leather.

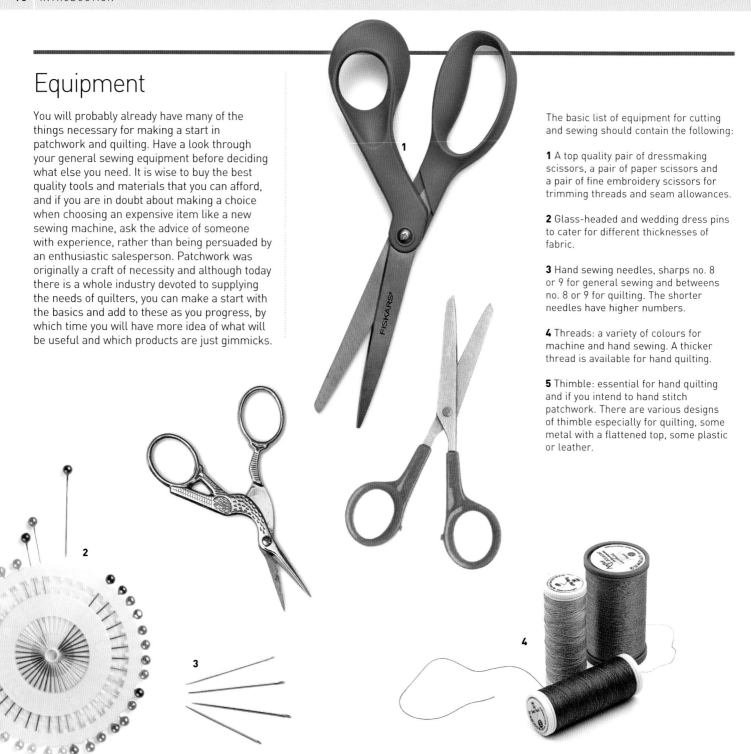

6 A beeswax cake prevents thread from knotting and strengthens it when hand-stitching.

7 Unpicker/seam ripper: useful for unpicking small stitches.

8 Steam iron for well-pressed patches and seams (not shown).

9 A sewing machine is essential for some types of patchwork, such as Seminole and String patchwork, and will speed up the process of construction in block patchwork (not shown).

10 Fabric marker: there are many on the market, find one which will draw a fine line.

11 Quilter's quarter: a small square plastic ruler 0.75 cm (¼ in) thick on all sides. Made of perspex, this is useful for checking seam allowances when making templates (not shown).

12 Tape measure with metric and imperial measures.

13 Rotary cutter: this is optional but will speed up the cutting out process considerably (see page 40).

14 Omnigrid ruler for rotary cutting.

15 Hera marker, which leaves an indented groove on the fabric, is an alternative to marker pen (not shown).

5

6

12

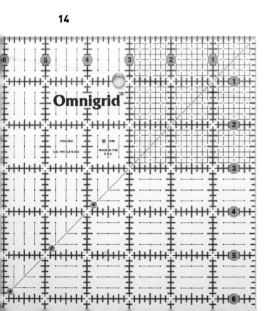

14

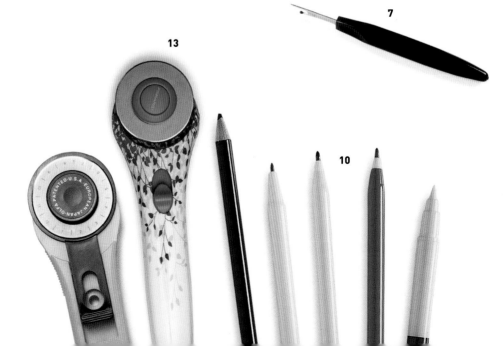

13

7

10

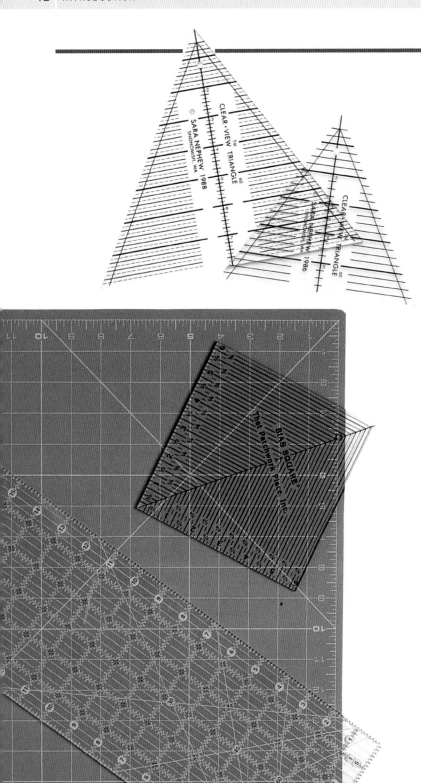

Templates and stencils

Templates and stencils are the master patterns for patchwork, appliqué and quilting. For hand-stitched patchwork and appliqué they are the finished size of the patch. As the fabric is cut a seam allowance is added all round. There are many commercially available templates or you can make your own by drawing the block full size, cutting out one of each of the shapes necessary for the design and gluing them onto stiff card or template plastic. When making your own templates make every effort to be absolutely accurate; mistakes at this stage will affect subsequent processes. Use a fine pencil with a sharp point.

For pieced blocks use graph paper to ensure accuracy in drawing the angles. If seam allowance has been added to the template as for machine-pieced blocks, shapes can be drawn edge to edge on the fabric. When marking round templates or stencils onto fabric for either appliqué or pieced patchwork, choose a fabric marker with which you can make a fine line to maintain accuracy.

Where appropriate, mark the fabric grain line on templates. This should run vertically and horizontally through the blocks.

Templates for appliqué
These can be drawn freehand or traced from patterns. Make them from stiff card or template plastic. Turnings are added as fabric is cut so the templates need to be the exact size and shape of the patch.

Templates for pieced patchwork
For hand stitching a line is drawn all round these templates onto the wrong side of the fabric to act as a guideline when stitching the patches together. Seam allowance is added as the fabric is cut, so leave enough space between shapes to allow for this.

Templates for patchwork
For machine-stitching draw templates as for hand stitching and mount them onto card or plastic, then add 0.75-cm (¼-in) seam allowance all round each piece before cutting them out. A quilter's quarter makes it easy to add the seam allowances. Mount the paper onto the base card or plastic, then butt the quilter's quarter against the edges of the paper and draw a fine line all round to cut out on. This will give the correct seam allowance of 0.75 cm (¼ in).

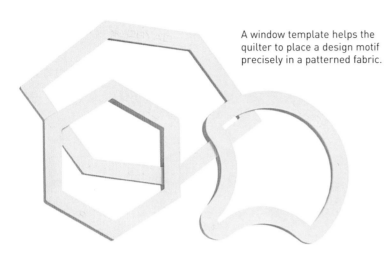

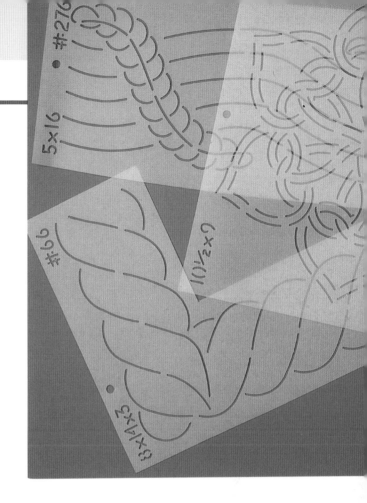

A window template helps the quilter to place a design motif precisely in a patterned fabric.

Window templates

These enable you to frame a specific part of the fabric to position a motif. The inner shape is the finished patch size cut out to create a window. An outer frame of 0.75 cm (¼ in) makes it possible to draw both the stitching and the cutting lines.

Where appropriate, mark the fabric grain line on templates. This should run vertically and horizontally through the blocks.

Quilting stencils

For elaborate quilting designs such as cables, shells and feathers etc., you will need to use quilting stencils. These should be made of a durable material such as cardboard, plastic or metal.

When using the stencil, you need to mark carefully round the outside and through the channels cut in the templates. If the design is repeated, you need to indicate the position where it overlaps by making a dot or notch on the template.

Far left, above and below: Examples of the different types of templates, stencils and measuring tools available.

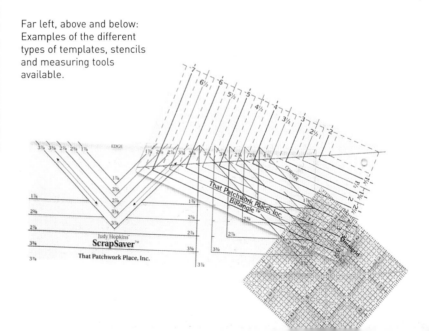

Materials

Suitable fabrics for quiltmaking include pure cotton in dress or light furnishing weight, lawn, poplin and polycotton. Corduroy and needlecord can also be used and their one-way pile or nap will give some interesting effects. Always wash fabrics separately before using them to shrink and test for dye fastness. If dye leaks out, continue to rinse until the water runs clear. If you are using old garments, cut away and discard any worn or faded parts. Avoid knitted fabrics as these will distort the fit of the patches and spoil the design. Exotic fabrics such as silk, velvet and taffeta can also be used, but may not be practical for items in everyday use – save these for decorative wall hangings and cushions, which need less cleaning. A visit to a quilt shop will demonstrate the wide range of plain and patterned fabrics available to the aspiring quiltmaker. Many shops also do mail order, some boasting over 1,000 prints and plains. Study the small ads in a needlework or quilt magazine to identify your nearest stockist. Apart from fabrics for the top, a quilt must also have a filler, the warm interlining known as wadding or batting, and backing fabric to enclose it.

A RANGE OF FABRICS
Different weights, different fibres, contrasting and complementary colours.

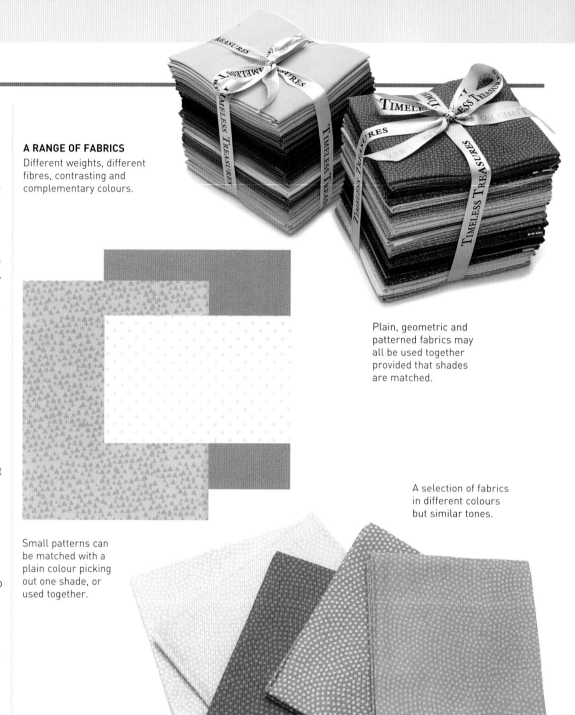

Plain, geometric and patterned fabrics may all be used together provided that shades are matched.

A selection of fabrics in different colours but similar tones.

Small patterns can be matched with a plain colour picking out one shade, or used together.

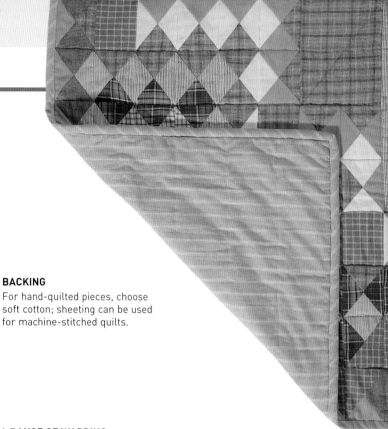

Wadding

Wadding is a very important part of the quilt and needs to be selected carefully. Many different materials are available to suit a quilt's particular purpose.

Polyester This is a man-made fibre available in different thicknesses known by weight, 60g (2 oz) being the thinnest and progressing to the thicker weights of 115g, 180g and 220g (4oz, 6oz and 8 oz). This is the most economical filler. Choose 60g (2 oz) for stitched quilting; the thicker ones are easier to tie quilt.

Cotton This is available in two forms: pure cotton, which must be closely quilted or it will 'migrate', that is move between the quilt top and backing and form lumps, and mixtures – one is called Cotton Classic – which contain some polyester and are easier to handle.

Domette This is a woven interlining. It is used to give wall hangings a flatter look which makes them hang well.

Needlepunch This is a polyester filler which has been flattened. Again, it is suitable for wall hangings.

Silk This is used to give a quilt or garment a luxury feel. Rather expensive and perhaps best reserved for small projects using silk fabrics.

New products appear regularly so check the manufacturer's advertisements. Sometimes you will see the term 'low loft' with regard to wadding. This means that the wadding is a flatter one which gives a less puffy appearance to the quilt.

Backing The backing on a quilt is usually a whole piece of fabric although 'Back Art' is a recent movement towards making the back of the quilt worthy of attention. For a hand-quilted back choose soft cottons which will be easy to stitch through. Sheeting can be used for machine quilting. Stitches will be less visible on patterned fabric than on plain. All fabrics used in a quilt should be similar in weight and fibre content. Using a thick, heavy fabric such as corduroy next to a fine lawn, for example, is not recommended.

BACKING
For hand-quilted pieces, choose soft cotton; sheeting can be used for machine-stitched quilts.

A RANGE OF WADDING
Various types of wadding are available, each with different qualities and applications.

Working it out

Once a decision has been made about the block designs to be used, consider how you want to join the blocks. You should also think about using sashing or not, and whether you wish to add a border.

Stitching the blocks together edge to edge will create secondary designs which appear between the blocks. These may be complex geometric patterns made by the shapes at the edges of the blocks merging together. Even seemingly simple blocks can have surprises in store when treated in this way. Lay out the blocks on a large, flat surface and check that unwanted or unattractive secondary designs are not going to be created before joining them.

Blocks that need to be separated can be set apart with sashing strips. Sashing will also increase the size of the quilt top. Make a sketch of the quilt top with the number of blocks, sizes and the arrangement of the sashing strips to work out the necessary widths and lengths required.

Pieced borders must be designed and planned in the same way as the quilt blocks. Draw a section of the quilt to its actual size, with enough of the border to establish the required sizes of the pieces, and make templates if necessary. Piece the border and attach it to the sides, top and bottom of the quilt, matching points and corners where appropriate.

PATCHWORK BLOCKS

Patchwork blocks all essentially break down into smaller units, i.e. four patch, nine patch, etc. Many blocks have traditionally been made as 12-inch blocks since 12 is divisible by 3 and 4. Therefore, when using metric measurements it is advisable to choose a block size that has this ease of divisibility, for example 24 cm. Many people working patchwork by hand mark the sewing line and then judge the seam allowance by eye, but if you intend to use a sewing machine an accurate cutting line including all seam allowances must be made.

METRIC AND IMPERIAL CONVERSIONS

Metric tools are now available. To avoid an array of heavily marked lines they are not marked every millimetre, but in intervals of 0.25 cm. Seam allowances therefore have to be carefully selected. If you were to take the straight conversion of the seam allowance being 6 mm you would find yourself having to cut shapes that have 1.2 cm added. This cannot be found on the rulers available. It has therefore been internationally recognized amongst patchworkers and the manufacturers of metric equipment that the standard seam allowance for patchwork using metric measurements is 0.75 cm. It is important that you sew an accurate 0.75 cm. This can be achieved by placing a masking-tape guide on the bed of your machine.

It is very important to follow either the metric or the imperial measurements given in this book. These have been calculated carefully to work for each quilting pattern and may not correspond to the conventional metric/imperial conversions.

FAIRFIELD PROCESSING CORP. GROUP QUILT
QUILTING THROUGH THE CENTURY
165 x 203 cm (65 x 80 in)

Estimating fabric

1 Make a sketch design of the entire quilt on graph paper with the correct number of blocks and any sashing strips and borders required.

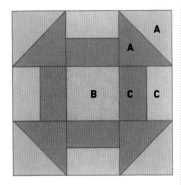

2 Decide on the number of different fabrics to be used in the blocks and draw a detailed plan of one block to indicate which fabrics will go where.

3 Count how many pieces of each shape will be required for one block. Multiply these totals by the number of blocks in the quilt to give the number of pieces needed overall in each different fabric and shape.

Measure the width of each type of fabric to be used and deduct 5 cm (2 in) to account for the selvedge. Work out how many pieces can be cut across the width. Divide the complete number of pieces needed in a particular fabric by the number that can be cut from each width of the fabric and multiply the depth of the template by the answer. Round up this last figure to the nearest 25 cm (¼ yd) to estimate the amount of this type of fabric needed.

4 For the sashing, look at the sketch design, and count the number of strips required. For example, in the chart on the left, 19 sashing strips are needed, 16 horizontal and 3 vertical. Work out their length and width. Repeat the calculation for the four strips – two for the width and two for the depth – to make up the borders. Add 5 cm (2 in) to the depth for seam allowance and estimate yardage required for both sashing and borders. It is important that sashing and borders are cut on the lengthwise grain of the fabric.

Templates

For appliqué templates calculate to the nearest geometric shape. It is sensible to buy extra yardage to allow for mistakes; if it is not used for the intended project, it can be saved and built up into a collection for future scrap quilts and smaller items.

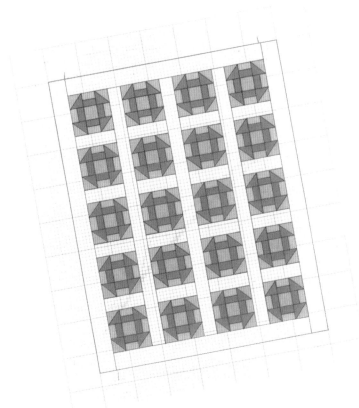

		1 Block	20 Blocks
	A (Triangles)	4	80
	C (Rectangles)	4	80
	A (Triangles)	4	80
	B (Squares)	1	20
	C (Rectangles)	4	80

Techniques

Although patchwork and quilting have their origins in economy and thrift, their decorative aspects have always been acknowledged. The versatility of patchwork and quilting lies to a great extent in the variety of techniques which comprise the craft. This section discusses projects suitable for all levels of ability, from simple pieced block designs for the beginner experimenting with colour, pattern and texture to more complex challenges for the experienced needleworker. As skills and confidence increase with practice, it will become clear that the diverse fabrics and stitching techniques presented here can provide a fascinating opportunity to express individual creativity. Both the traditional techniques, such as 'English' or mosaic patchwork, block patchwork and appliqué, and more recent developments using rotary cutters and sewing machines, are considered in the following pages.

Blocks

■■■ ■ ■ ■ ■ ■ ■ ■ ■ ■ ■ ■ ■ ■ ■ ■ ■

Blocks consist of a repeated unit of shapes which when stitched together, form the basis of a quilt design. From early beginnings when simple one-patch patterns involving squares, rectangles or diamonds made full use of scrap bag fabrics, designs were invented and refined, often by folding paper into four or nine equal divisions of a square, then subdividing the resulting grid into further geometric shapes – smaller squares, triangles or rhomboids. This formed the basis of block design. Although originally brought from Europe, it was explored and extended by American quilters who made it uniquely their own.

As the construction of each individual block had the advantage of economy in both materials and space, it had much to recommend it to the early settlers, for whom both were in short supply. Only when enough blocks were finished to make the quilt top was more room needed to assemble, quilt and finish the piece. These later stages of the quilt were often done quickly as a co-operative effort at a quilting bee.

Both pieced patchwork and appliqué can be made in block format and often the two techniques are combined in designs such as Carolina Lily or the numerous basket blocks. Block patterns were often identified by names which referred to local and national

events, stories from the Bible or characters from public life, for example Flying Geese, Sherman's March and Jacob's Ladder. To some extent block names were dependent on locale; the same block is known variously as Duck's Foot in the Mud, Hand of Friendship and Bear's Paw.

Block patterns

Block patterns fall into different categories. The one patch uses just one single shape, but within this limitation order can be imposed by organising the colours and values to create designs. A good example is the Thousand Pyramids block, which uses equilateral triangles. By the simple device of placing all the dark triangles pointing upwards and all the light ones downwards, the dark triangles combine to give the illusion in the name.

Sets of blocks containing a combination of shapes take their name from the grid which can be imposed over the design. Four patch and nine patch are the most numerous, but there are also many irregular blocks. By breaking down the block into its basic grid you can determine the order of construction. Start with the smallest pieces and wherever possible work in straight lines.

Secondary patterns

It is only when you start placing blocks edge to edge that the secondary designs begin to appear. The shapes merge together to form a complex overall design and frequently make it difficult to identify the individual block. Once this concept is understood, it can be exploited to dynamic effect by the careful choice of colours, textures and values in the fabrics used.

If, rather than create these secondary designs, you want to preserve the identity of individual block patterns, they can be separated by sashing, strips of fabric often in plain colours which divide the blocks and give a lattice effect. This technique is often used with album quilts, those in which each block is different. To set such blocks edge to edge would create a confused jumble.

By turning the block into a diamond shape, or setting it 'on point', a totally different effect can be achieved. In this case the edges of the quilt must be filled with triangles to finish the square or rectangular shape.

From simple beginnings, infinite possibilities have been developed and remain to be explored.

Three types of block pattern, used in quilts made by Katharine Guerrier. From far left to right: Jacob's Ladder, Thousand Pyramids and a secondary pattern, formed by the careful juxtaposition of individual blocks.

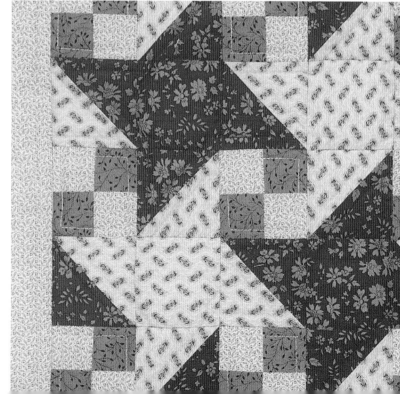

Block Construction

Although sewing machines are now frequently considered a normal part of household equipment, many people still prefer to sew patchwork by hand. Quilters give various reasons: the fact that it makes a project more portable, with the advantage of being able to sit with the family while working on a quilt, or the slower pace of construction which gives time for making decisions about what colour or where to put the next piece of fabric, or even for the sheer nostalgic value which somehow puts them in spiritual contact with quiltmakers from a previous era. If you want fast results, however, a machine-sewn quilt is a more realistic proposition. Many contemporary quilters combine the two by machine piecing and hand quilting; no machine can emulate the unique properties of beautiful hand quilting.

Hand sewing

If hand sewing you will need to mark the stitching line by drawing round the templates on the wrong side of the fabric. Add in the seam allowance before you cut out the patches. Begin and end stitching at each seam line (not the edge of the fabric), starting with a small knot or backstitch and ending firmly with a backstitch. Press seams to one side – where possible the darker side.

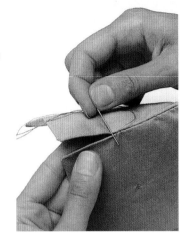

Machine sewing

When sewing patches together by machine it is not necessary to mark a stitching line. Just place the patches right sides together, pin, then guide the raw edges of the fabric against the presser foot of the machine. The foot on most sewing machines will automatically give 0.75 cm (¼ in) seam allowance. If yours does not, mark the plate on your machine with a narrow strip of masking tape parallel to the seam line 0.75 cm (¼ in) from the needle. Alternatively, check out whether the 'Little Foot' developed especially for patchwork will fit your machine. This will measure the seam allowance for you at exactly 0.75 cm (¼ in) from the edge.

Basic piecing techniques

1 Chain piecing is a quick way of piecing together a quantity of patches.

Place the patches right sides together and sew with a running stitch by hand or machine.

2 Cut chain-pieced patches apart and press seams. Machine-sewn seams are strong enough to be pressed open, or they can be pressed to one side.

Piecing order

It is important to ensure that all the patches are organized in the correct order before any stitching takes place.

1 When all the patches are cut out, spread them out on a flat surface in the correct position. Make up the squares.

3 Join the rows to form one block.

2 Set the squares together in rows.

NANCY BRELAND,
MOSAIC (DETAIL)
Accurate piecing of the blocks in the quilt contribute to the complex secondary designs.

Setting in

Stitch straight lines where possible. Some blocks, however, need to have pieces 'set in' to a right-angled corner.

1 Stitch the first seam up to the 0.75-cm (¼-in) seam allowance to create the right angle.

3 Press the seam away from the set-in patch.

2 Stitch the piece to be set in along one edge, then pivot through the right angle and stitch along the other edge.

4 The finished unit seen from the front.

Piecing angled shapes

When joining shapes that have angles other than 90 degrees – diamonds and triangles – align the stitching lines, *not* the cut edges. This makes a straight edge when the patches are opened.

Matching points

Many blocks have a point at which four or more different fabrics meet.

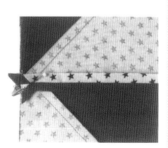

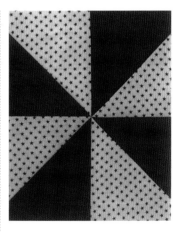

1 To match these points accurately, push a pin through at the exact spot where the points are to be matched, at a right angle to the stitching line. Stitch up to the pin.

2 Carefully remove the pin, then stitch over the point.

Piecing curved seams

If the block has curved seams, as in the Drunkard's Path pattern, concave and convex edges must be joined.

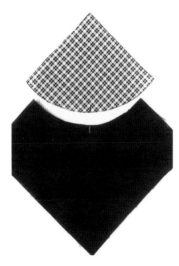

1 Cut pieces and mark the centre points. Clip into the concave curve within the 0.75-cm (¼-in) seam allowance (no more than 0.375 cm (⅛ in).

3 Sew along the stitching line by hand or machine with the concave curved piece on top and keeping the raw edges together as you sew.

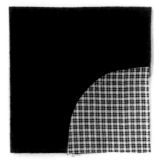

2 Pin these centre points and the ends together, then ease the curves to fit, putting in several pins to hold them in place.

4 Press seams towards the patch with the convex curve.

JOSEPHINE KNOT

This complex-looking design is made from four sections. These are combined in diagonals to form the final design.

Four-Patch Blocks

The most effective solution to a design problem is often the simplest, and the four-patch block has the virtue of simplicity built into its structure. The basic block is just what its name suggests; four equal-sized squares of fabric stitched together. To make the block more complex, these squares can be subdivided within the grid. The Pinwheel and Broken Dishes blocks have the squares divided into half-square triangles. The composition of the four-patch block for the Pinwheel pattern is shown in detail on these two pages. By contrast, the Big Dipper and Hovering Hawks blocks use quarter squares. A darker rectangle cuts diagonally across each of the four equal squares in Devil's Puzzle, and in the Robbing Peter to Pay Paul block, curved seams and reverse colour values give a counterchange effect.

Star blocks are always popular and two which fall into the four-patch family are Ribbon Star and Pierced Star. There are dozens of other four-patch blocks, some of which become subdivided into 4 x 4 or even 8 x 8 equal divisions, but as long as it is possible to impose an equal 2 x 2 grid over a design, it is a four patch.

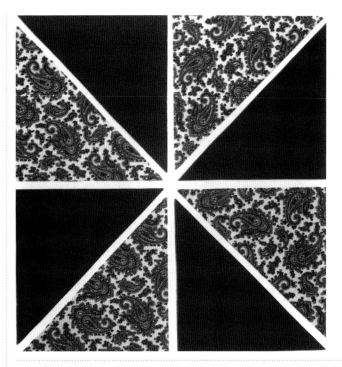

Constructing a four-patch block
1 Place patches in the required position on a flat surface.

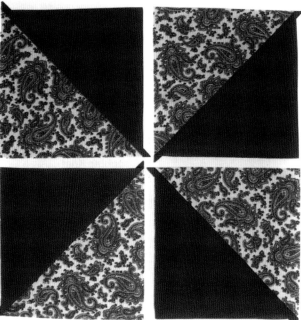

2 Join the triangles first to make four squares. Seams can be pressed open or to one side.

3 Next, join the squares to make two rectangles, matching the points.

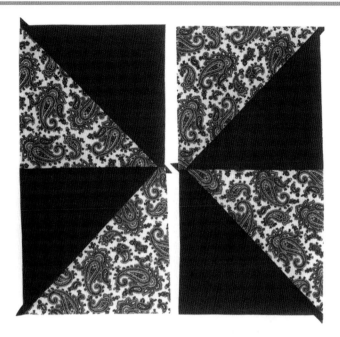

4 Finally, join the two rectangles to make the square, matching the points of the centre of the block.

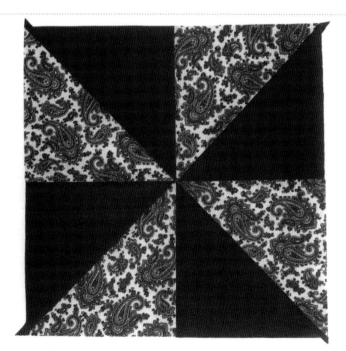

Four-Patch Blocks

BIG DIPPER

The contrast between light and dark creates the counterchange in the design.

BROKEN DISHES

Dark, medium and light values are used in this simple block.

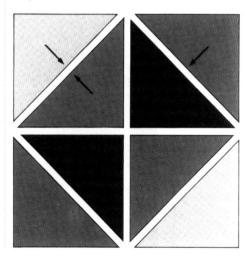

DEVIL'S PUZZLE

Placed edge to edge, the blocks in this design will create
a strong secondary design with diagonal emphasis.

ROBBING PETER TO PAY PAUL

A four-patch block which makes use of
curved seams.

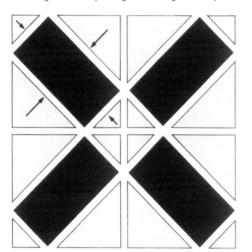

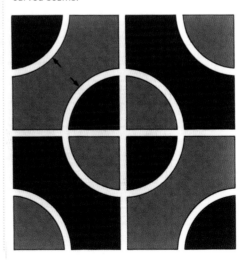

Nine-Patch Blocks

As its name suggests, the nine-patch block is divided into a 3 x 3 grid. Examples of this type that are simple to piece include Friendship Star, Shoofly and Ohio Star. The composition of the nine-patch block for the Shoofly pattern is shown in detail on these two pages. A vast variety of different designs can be created by dividing the grid in more complex ways, some presenting more of a challenge than others. Card Trick, for example, uses the juxtaposition of different colours to create a three-dimensional effect. Secondary designs are also important in many nine-patch block quilts, as in the intriguingly titled Contrary Wife. Whatever your choice, plan the design with consideration of the tonal values of the fabrics to be used. Placing the emphasis on another part of a block can make it look completely different. Try shading the same block design in different tonal combinations. The results are often surprising.

Some of the most interesting nine-patch blocks are featured on the following pages.

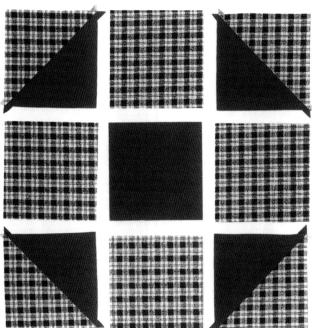

Constructing a nine-patch block
1 Arrange the patches in the required order on a flat surface.

2 Join the triangles to form squares. Press seams open or to the darker side.

3 Stitch the squares into three rows as shown.

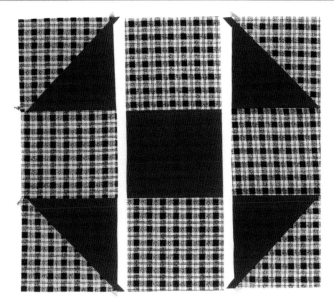

4 Stitch the three rows together to make up the block.

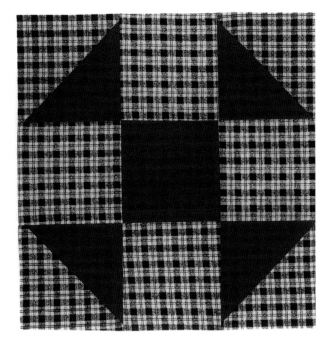

Nine-Patch Blocks

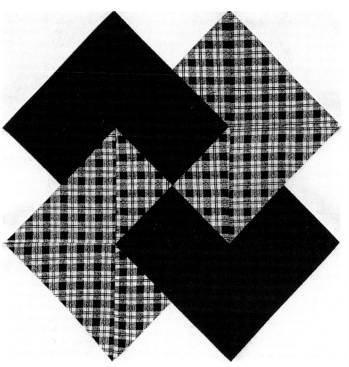

CARD TRICK
This block has an intriguing three-dimensional effect created by placement of dark, medium and light fabrics.

PALM LEAF
One of a number of 'leaf' blocks.

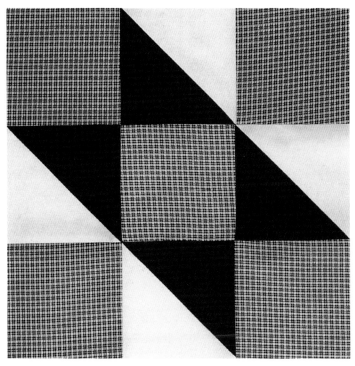

CONTRARY WIFE

Strong secondary designs emerge when blocks are placed edge to edge.

FIFTY-FOUR FORTY OR FIGHT

This interesting title refers to the dispute between the United States and British Canada over the division of the Pacific Northwest in 1846.

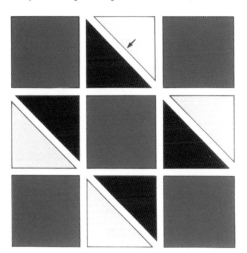

Irregular Blocks

The whole area of block classification can be confusing when you start to study patchwork; even within the simpler categories of four- and nine-patch blocks, there is some overlap. For this reason the blocks which cannot easily be fitted into either of these sets are here termed as 'irregular' blocks. By analyzing the shapes within the block and determining the grid which fits over the block – whether it be equal units of 5 x 5, 7 x 7 or any other combination, it becomes clear how the pieces will fit together and how the block can be constructed. The same rules apply: smaller shapes combine to make larger ones, and sew in straight lines wherever this is possible.

CAKE STAND

This is a popular 'picture' block because the design is simple and good for using up scraps.

JOSEPHINE KNOT

This block is split diagonally with each quarter section made up of only three pieces.

OLD MAID'S RAMBLE
Fragmented triangles in opposing values create the counterchange effect.

ASYMMETRICAL BLOCKS
These can be designed within the framework of any grid.

Log Cabin

A favourite among the traditional designs, Log Cabin quilts are often seen to have a significance beyond their qualities of graphic design, representing home in the hostile conditions faced by the pioneers.

Although Log Cabin quilts were known to have been made in Europe, the design is largely associated with the early settlers in the United States and it has maintained its popularity up to the present day. The construction of the Log Cabin block is straightforward; strips of fabric rotate around a centre square, traditionally red to represent the fire or hearth. The block is split diagonally into light and dark fabrics to create the illusion of shadows and flickering firelight within the cabin. There are variations to this basic pattern but they all rely on the visual play of light and dark tonal values. Although a single block looks simple, the versatility of the design can only be realized when the blocks are placed together in multiples and their secondary designs become apparent. Dozens of different variations are possible, all with great visual impact and all of which exploit the contrast between the dark and light fabrics with graphic simplicity.

There are many named designs such as Barn Raising and Sunshine and Shadows plus numerous others which can all be made by using combinations of the basic block.

Construction

Traditionally the block is stitched onto a square of foundation fabric – this stabilises the fabrics and encloses the seams on the back. Decide on the finished size of your block; 30 to 38 cm (12 to 15 in) would be suitable for a quilt, a panel of four blocks 20 to 23 cm (8 to 9 in) square would make a cushion front. Plan the design on graph paper to determine measurements. Three factors will affect the finished size of the block: the dimensions of the centre square, the width of the strips and how many rounds of strips are used.

1 Cut a square of foundation fabric – white sheeting or calico – about 4 cm (1½ in) larger than the desired finished size of the block. Press diagonal creases with a steam iron, then place the centre square right side up on the foundation square, with the corners aligned on the diagonal creases.

2 This ensures that the block centre is positioned in the middle of the foundation square.

3 Sort the fabrics into light and dark colours. All pieces – centres and strips – can be cut with the rotary cutting set. Add seam allowances as you cut. For a 5-cm (2-in) finished centre square cut 6.5 x 6.5 cm (2½ x 2½ in). For 2.5 cm (1 in) finished strips cut strips 4 cm (1½ in) wide.

Select a different coloured fabric from the lighter pile. Cut a strip the desired width and the length of one side of the centre square. Place this right side down on the centre square, raw edges together. Pin and stitch through the three layers taking a 0.75-cm (¼-in) seam allowance.

4 Turn the strip over to reveal the right side of the fabric and then press flat against the foundation.

5 Turn the foundation square through 90 degrees anticlockwise, and place the second strip – using the same fabric – right side down against the centre and short edge of the first strip. Align the raw edges, then stitch down through all layers as before. Fold this strip back and press.

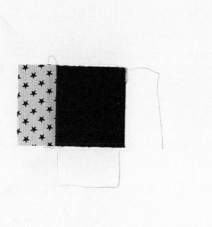

6 Turn the foundation through another 90 degrees anticlockwise, then select a fabric from a contrasting, darker pile. Cut a strip and add this to the block in the same way. Turn and press flat against the foundation.

7 The fourth strip completes the first round. This will establish which is to be the dark side of the block and which the light side.

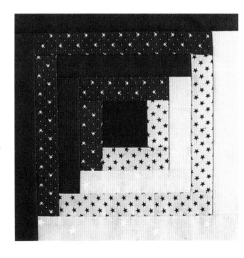

8 Continue to add strips, maintaining the correct light/dark sequence until the block is complete. (The sequence for arranging the steps is shown in the numbered diagram, right). Trim away the foundation to the edges of the last round of strips, leaving 0.75-cm (¼-in) seam allowance all round for joining the blocks together. Arrange the blocks in the design required, and place them right sides together, then stitch through all layers taking a 0.75-cm (¼-in) seam allowance.

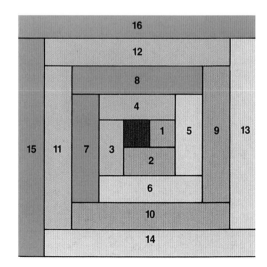

COURTHOUSE STEPS

In this variation, strips are sewn on opposite sides of the centre square in an alternate dark/light sequence, so that a quite different effect is achieved. This pattern is sometimes also known as Chinese Lanterns.

BARN RAISING

Another arrangement of the blocks which results in concentric diamonds of alternating dark and light coloured fabrics.

SUNSHINE AND SHADOW

The width of the strips can be varied. In this version the lighter coloured strips are wider than the dark ones, giving the effect of curved lines. The Sunshine and Shadow design can also be done with strips of the same width.

Rotary Cutting

□□□□□□□□□□□□□□□□□□□□□□□

Making Basic Shapes

Speed-Piecing

Seminole Patchwork

String Patchwork

The pressures of modern living have brought demands to speed up the process of quiltmaking. The introduction of rotary cutting has eliminated much of the time spent cutting the patches. Templates are not used for rotary cutting – except for curved seams – and seam allowances are included in the overall dimensions of the pieces when they are cut.

Metric rotary-cutting
There is no direct conversion between metric and imperial measurements for rotary cutting. Different rulers are available for each system.

Strips, squares and rectangles have a 0.75 cm (¼ in)seam allowance. For half square triangles add 2.5 cm (1 in)to the finished size before cutting the square in half, for quarter-square triangles add 3.5 cm (1⅜ in) to the finished size before cutting the square in four.

The rotary-cutting set
Although there are many tools and rulers available, everything can be done with just a few tools. The four essentials are a rotary cutter, a board, a square and a ruler. The rotary cutter is a circular blade set in a handle with a safety lock. It is important to get into the habit of using this lock each time that you put the cutter down. The board is made from a score-resistant material which will not blunt the blade and comes in a variety of sizes. The ruler is made of thick clear plastic with a straight, non-bevelled edge and also comes in a variety of sizes.

A good basic set would include a large rotary cutter, a board 60 x 46 cm (24 x 18 in), and a ruler 15 x 60 cm (6 x 24 in). In addition you need a square; a 15-cm (6-in) bias square is the most useful.

With this equipment you will be able to cut and subcut strips into many geometrical shapes. However, to be successful you need to use the equipment accurately and safely. The ruler and the board are marked with a grid but you are advised to use the grid on the ruler and not that on the board. The ruler is laser printed but the board is printed with the use of rollers and can, on some occasions, be inaccurate. To save confusion use the board plain side up.

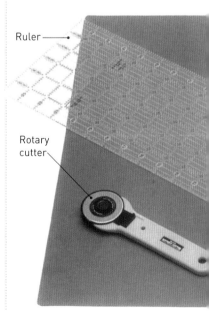

Ruler ——

Rotary cutter

Setting up and squaring the fabric

1 Place the washed and ironed fabric on the board with the fold towards you and the selvedges away from you. Any surplus fabric should lie away to the side of your cutting hand. Place the square on the folded edge of the fabric close to the edge that you will cut. Place the ruler next to the square with one of the horizontal lines on the edge of the fabric. The edge of the ruler should butt up to the square. Hold the ruler down firmly and slide the square away.

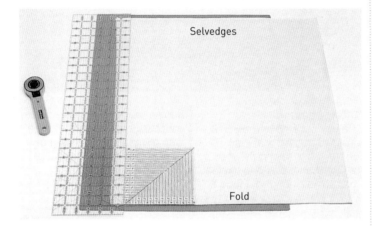

Selvedges

Fold

Cutting board   Square

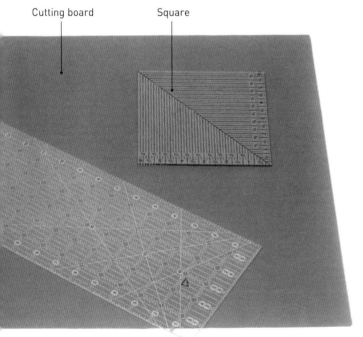

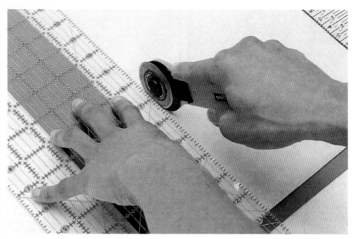

2 Holding the ruler steady, open the cutter and place the blade next to the ruler. Start cutting, pushing the cutter firmly away from you with an even pressure as you do so. When the cutter comes level with your hand, stop cutting but maintain the pressure.

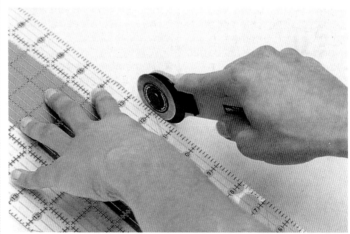

3 Move your hand up the ruler to a new position and then cut again to a point level with your hand. Keep repeating until you reach the selvedges. Remember to only move one hand at a time, either the one cutting or the one holding the ruler. This initial squaring-up cut is the only time that you cut through only the two thicknesses of fabric.

Making Basic Shapes

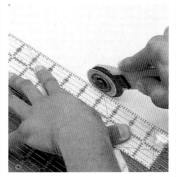

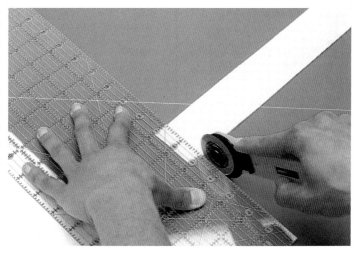

Cutting strips

1 Fold the fabric over in half again so that the folded edge is positioned on top of the selvedges and all the cut edges match.

2 To cut a strip place a horizontal line on the fold of the fabric and the line indicating your desired width along the cut edges. Keeping a horizontal line on the fold at all times will prevent you from cutting strips with 'V' shapes at the folds. When the ruler is in the correct position, hold the ruler in place with your hand – firmly splayed in the middle of your ruler – and cut with the blade against the ruler. Starting ahead of the fold, cut with an even pressure across the fabric. If you are going to subcut these strips, leave them folded.

Cutting squares

1 Take a cut strip and place it across the board with the double fold to the right if you are right-handed and to the left if you are left-handed. Place a horizontal line of the ruler on the lower edge of the strip and cut a small strip from the selvedge edge to straighten the end of the strip.

2 Place a horizontal line on the edge of the strip and the vertical line of the square measurement along the straightened end of the strip and cut the square. You will have four in a stack. Repeat the square cutting until you have the required amount. If necessary you may need to straighten the vertical edge again occasionally.

3 Remember when cutting strips to add a seam allowance of 0.75 cm (¼ in) to each side of the strip before you cut.

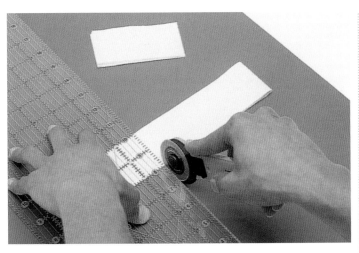

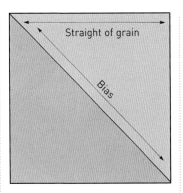

Subcutting into rectangles

1 Position the ready-cut strip on the board and straighten the end as you did for a square. Then, with a horizontal line on the lower edge and the vertical measurement on the straightened edge, cut a rectangle from the strip.

Subcutting into half-square triangles

1 A half-square triangle is illustrated above. It is used whenever the shorter edges of the triangle are parallel to the edge of the block or quilt.

3 Cut a strip the width of the finished size of the triangle plus 2 cm (⅞ in) and cut a square the same width.

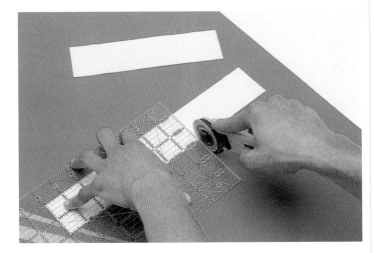

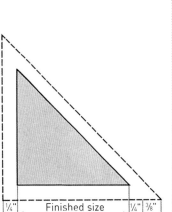

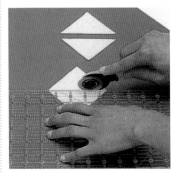

2 If the length of the rectangle is longer than the width of the ruler, simply turn the ruler through 90 degrees and use the other way round.

2 To cut a half-square triangle a square is cut and then cut again diagonally. So that sufficient fabric is allowed for seam allowances all round, it is important to consider the triangle drawn on graph paper. Add 0.75 cm (¼ in) all round and then measure the short side. It will be 2 cm (⅞ in) longer than the finished size of the triangle. Rule for half-square triangles: finished size plus 2 cm (⅞ in).

4 Place the ruler across the diagonal of the square and cut the stack of squares into two stacks of triangles. Repeat for more triangles.

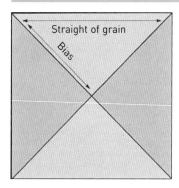

Subcutting into quarter-square triangles

1 A quarter-square triangle is illustrated above. It is used whenever the longer edge of the triangle is parallel to the edge of the block or quilt.

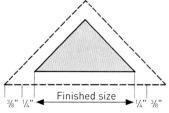

2 To make a quarter-square triangle a square is cut and then cut again on both diagonals. To ensure that sufficient fabric is allowed, it is worth looking at the triangle drawn on graph paper. Add 0.75 cm (¼ in) all round and then measure the long side. It will be 3 cm (1¼ in) longer than the finished size of the triangle.

Rule for quarter-square triangles: finished size plus 3 cm (1¼ in).

3 Cut a strip the width of the finished size of the triangle plus 3 cm (1¼ in) and cut a square the same width.

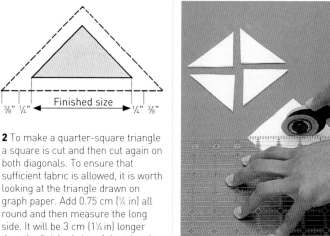

4 Place the ruler across the diagonal and cut. Do not move the pieces.

5 Place the ruler across the other diagonal and cut. You will now have four stacks of quarter-square triangles. Repeat the process for more triangles.

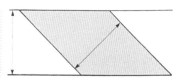

Subcutting into diamonds

1 Diamonds either have 45-degree or 60-degree angles. The distances between the parallel sides are always equal The strips that you cut are the same as the distance between the parallel sides plus the seam allowances.

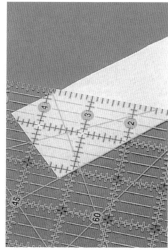

2 When the strip is cut, you need to set up the angle of 45 degrees at one end by pivoting the ruler until the 45-degree line lies along the bottom edge of the strip.

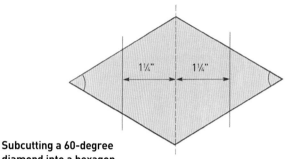

Subcutting a 60-degree diamond into a hexagon

1 First cut the diamonds. Let us assume the measurement used is 6 cm (2½ in).

3 To cut diamonds keep the 45-degree line on the bottom edge of the strip and slide the ruler across until the angled edge is on the line of the measurement of the strip. Repeat the process as necessary for more diamonds.

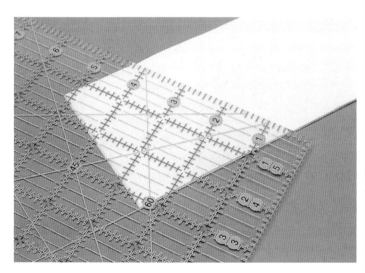

4 To cut 60-degree diamonds you should follow the same process. However, this time use the 60-degree line along the bottom edge of the strip.

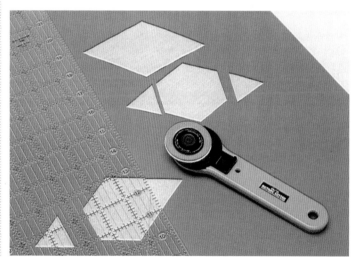

2 To change the diamond into a hexagon, cut the long points off. Measure half the original measurement (i.e. 3 cm/1¼ in) from the short diagonal and cut. Turn the diamond round and make the opposite cut the same way.

Subcutting strips into trapezoids

1 It can be seen from the diagram that the rule for a trapezoid with one point is the same as that for a half-square triangle: add 2 cm (⅞ in) to the finished size of the base.

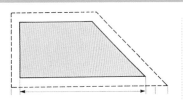

2 Using a strip that is the width of the trapezoid plus the seam allowances, straighten the left edge.

3 From the left edge measure the base measurement plus 2 cm (⅞ in). Mark a dot on the bottom edge of the strip.

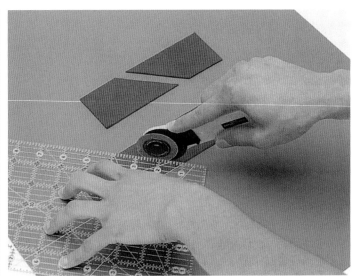

4 Placing the 45-degree line on the bottom edge of the strip and the edge of the ruler on the dot, cut at 45 degrees.

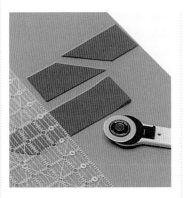

5 For the next cut measure the length of the trapezoid plus 2 cm (⅞ in) along the top edge of the strip and cut straight. You are then ready to repeat the process for more trapezoids.

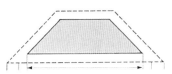

6 From the diagram you can see that the rule for a trapezoid with two points is the same as that for a quarter-square triangle: add 3 cm (1¼ in).

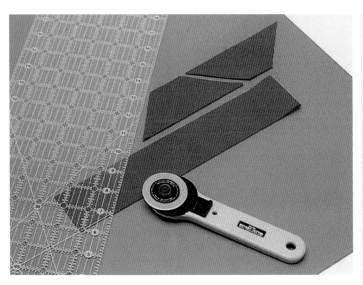

7 Using a strip the width of the trapezoid plus seam allowances with the 45-degree line on the bottom edge of the strip, cut the left-hand end at 45 degrees.

9 With the 45-degree line on the bottom edge of the strip and the edge of the ruler on the dot, cut at 45 degrees in the opposite direction to the first cut.

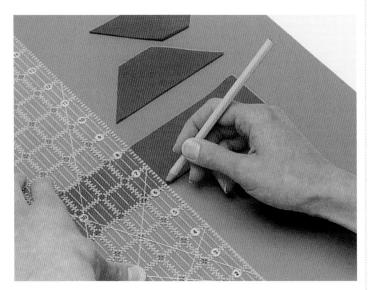

8 Measure along the bottom edge the length of the trapezoid plus 3 cm (1¼ in) and mark with a dot.

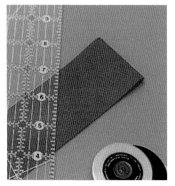

10 The point is established. Now measure the length of the base plus 3 cm (1¼ in) along the top edge of the strip. Mark with a dot.

11 Keeping the 45-degree line along the top edge and the edge of the ruler on the dot, cut at 45 degrees. Repeat the process for more trapezoids.

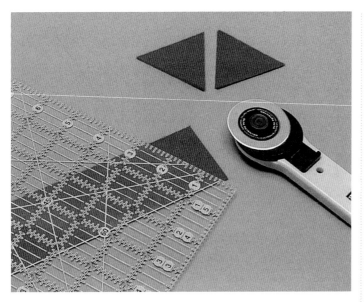

Subcutting squares into octagons

1 Using cut squares, mark lines diagonally across the square.

2 Measuring from the centre, cut the corner of the square off at a distance half the width of the original square.

Subcutting strips into 60-degree triangles

1 Using strips that are the width of the height of the triangle plus seam allowances, place the 60-degree line along the bottom edge of the strip. Cut out the strip at 60 degrees on the right-hand edge.

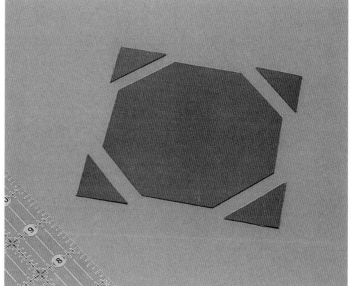

2 Pivot the ruler on the 60-degree line so that the other 60-degree line is now on the bottom edge of the strip and the edge of the ruler is on the top edge at the cut. Cut at 60 degrees.

3 Pivot the ruler again and you are ready to make the third cut. Repeat the process to produce more triangles.

3 Repeat for the other corners.

Speed-Piecing

Once you have mastered the rotary cutter there are many quilt patterns that can be cut and pieced quickly. For example Log Cabin blocks can be made more efficiently if you can cut straight strips. Some quilt designs require you to sew the strips together before you cut. The simplest of these is a Rail Fence, but there are many others such as simple four-patch, nine-patch, Irish Chain and Trip Around The World.

Most patchwork blocks break down into simple shapes that can be cut with the rotary cutter. If a quilt is made of lots of repeated blocks, it is best to do the cutting for all the blocks at once rather than one at a time. Also, when a design calls for many half-square triangles these can be created by using a 'Grid Method' to save time. However if you are only making one block you can use the method set out for the Friendship Star.

Nine-patch block

The measurements given here are for a 15-cm (6-in) finished block. To change the size of the block, determine the desired finished size of the patch and add 1.5 cm (½ in) to the width of the strips as you cut them. Use the same measurement as the width of the strips to cut the cross sections, e.g. for a 24-cm (9-in) block the patch measures 8 cm (3 in), so cut strips and sections 9 cm (3½ in) wide.

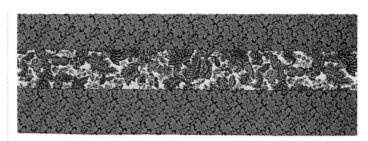

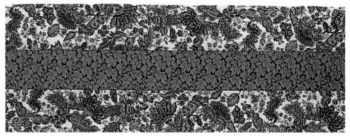

1 Cut three dark and three light strips – 6.5 cm (2½ in) wide across the width of the fabric. Seam them together (taking a 0.75-cm (¼-in) seam allowance) in two sets of three dark/light/dark and light/dark/light.

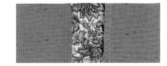

2 Press seams to one side – towards the centre strip on one set and away from the centre strip on the other. Place the two sets right sides together matching the seams. Straighten one short end, then cut into 6.5-cm (2½-in) strips across the seams.

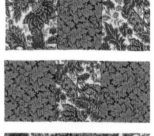

3 Arrange the desired nine-patch and stitch. The seams will match as they lock together.

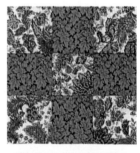

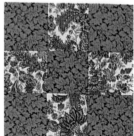

4 The final seams can be pressed open or to one side as preferred.

Pinwheel and Broken Dishes

The measurements given here are for a 15-cm (6-in) finished block. To change the size of the block add 2-cm (⅞ in) to the size of the finished unit when cutting the squares, e.g. for a 20-cm (8-in) block the unit would be 10-cm (4-in), so cut squares 12.5 cm (4⅞ in).

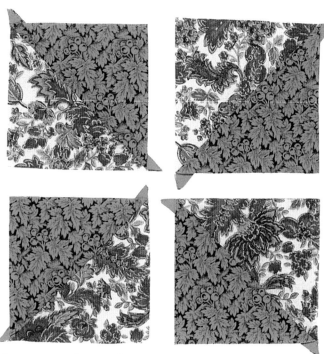

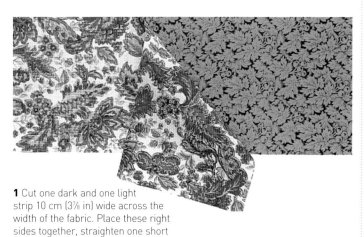

1 Cut one dark and one light strip 10 cm (3⅞ in) wide across the width of the fabric. Place these right sides together, straighten one short side and cut into four squares.

4 Press seams and arrange the resulting units in the desired block pattern.

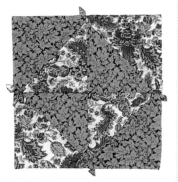

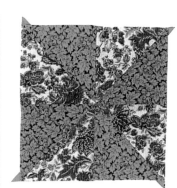

2 Mark one diagonal line on the wrong side of one of the fabric squares.

3 Taking a 0.75-cm (¼-in) seam allowance, sew on either side of the line and cut on the line.

Pinwheel

Broken Dishes

Letter X

Measurements given here are for a 15-cm (6-in) finished block. To change the size of the block, add 3 cm (1¼ in) to the finished size of the unit.

Many blocks are made from units of squares, rectangles, half-square triangles and quarter-square triangles, and they can all be constructed using quick piecing.

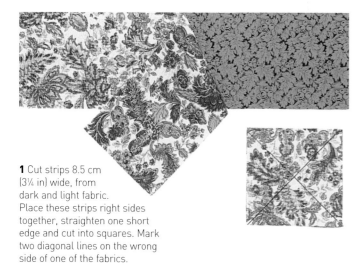

1 Cut strips 8.5 cm (3¼ in) wide, from dark and light fabric. Place these strips right sides together, straighten one short edge and cut into squares. Mark two diagonal lines on the wrong side of one of the fabrics.

3 One set of squares will make two units. Cut the plain squares 6.5 x 6.5 cm (2½ x 2½ in).

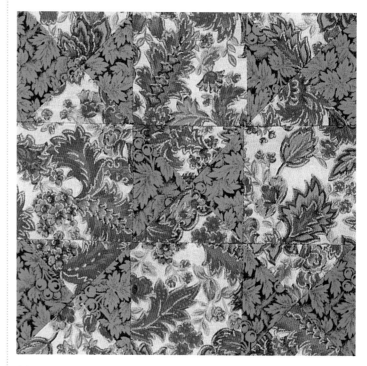

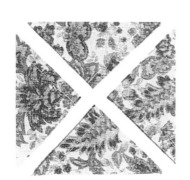

2 Stitch to the centre on the left-hand side of the lines, then cut along the drawn lines.

4 Arrange the units as shown above.

Ohio Star block

This block uses square and quarter-square triangle units. It is a nine-patch block. For a 30-cm (12-in) block, the size of the finished unit is 10 cm (4 in).

Cut the squares 11.5 x 11.5 cm (4½ x 4½ in), four light and one dark coloured. For the triangle units cut two dark coloured squares 13 x 13 cm (5¼ x 5¼ in) and two light coloured squares 13 x 13 cm (5¼ x 5¼ in). The squares are 3 cm (1¼ in) larger than the size of the finished unit.

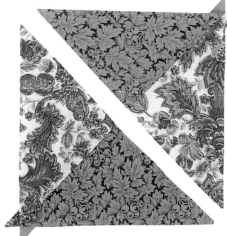

3 Two of the resulting triangles, each of which is made up of one each of equally sized dark and light triangles, can be seamed together to make one unit made of four half-square triangles.

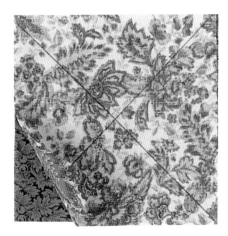

1 Place these squares right side together and steam press. Draw two diagonal lines across the square (on the wrong side of the farbic), dividing it into quarters, and sew 0.75 cm (¼ in) to the left of each line in each quarter, from the edge of the fabric to the point at which the lines cross.

2 Cut along the drawn diagonal lines, open out the resulting triangles and press flat.

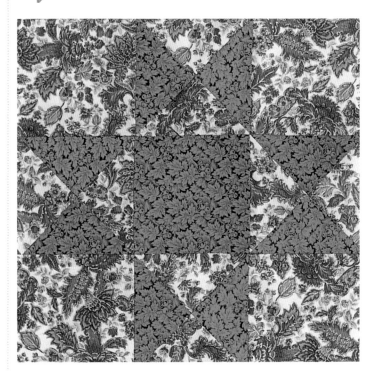

4 The complete Ohio Star block using quarter-square triangle units.

Friendship Star block

This block will require four light squares 11.5 x 11.5 cm (4½ x 4½ in) and one dark square 11.5 x 11.5 cm (4½ x 4½ in). For the triangle units, two light squares 12.5 x 12.5 cm (4⅞ x 4⅞ in). For squares or rectangles add 0.75 cm (¼ in) all round to the desired finished size of the shape. For half-square triangles add 2 cm (⅞ in) to the size of the square. For this block you will need two squares each of the dark and light fabric 12.5 x 12.5 cm (4⅞ x 4⅞ in).

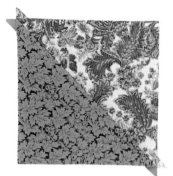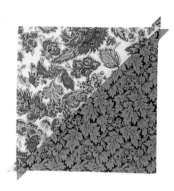

4 This will make two half-square triangle units 11.5 x 11.5 cm (4½ x 4½ in).

1 Place one dark and one light coloured square right sides together and steam press. Draw one diagonal line across the squares.

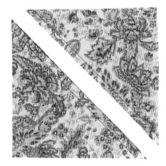

3 Cut along the drawn line.

2 Stitch on both sides of the line taking 0.75-cm (¼-in) seam allowance.

5 Arrange the units as illustrated with the squares to complete the block.

Flying Geese

If a different size unit is required, just cut the small squares into half the size of the large one and add 0.75 cm (¼ in).

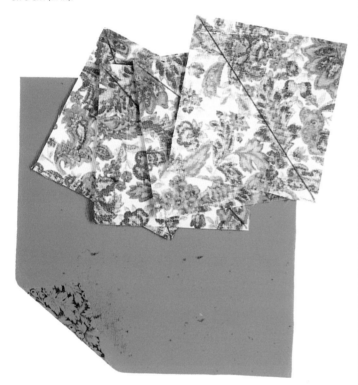

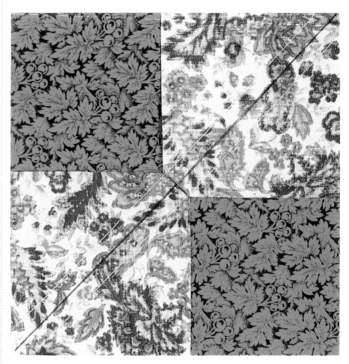

1 Cut one square of 'goose' fabric 15 x 15 cm (6 x 6 in) and four squares of background fabric 8.25 x 8.25 cm (3¼ x 3¼ in). Mark one diagonal line on each of the background squares on the wrong side of the fabric.

2 Lay the larger square flat, right side up and place one small square in the corner, right side down. Snip off the corner where it crosses the centre of the larger square. Pin another square in the opposite corner, trim the corner off this one also. Sew from corner to corner 0.75 cm (¼ in) on either side of the diagonal line.

4 Cut along both diagonals and press seams.

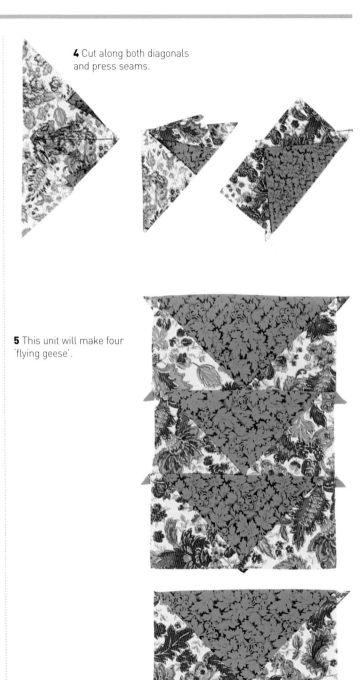

5 This unit will make four 'flying geese'.

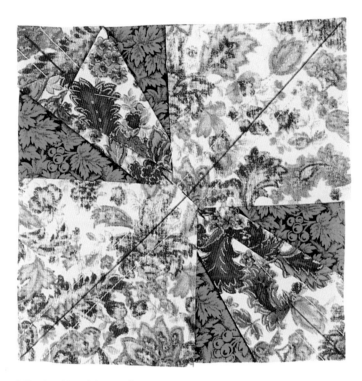

3 Pin the sides of the smaller squares away from the centre, place the other two smaller squares in the remaining corners and trim off the centre corners as before. Sew on either side of the marked diagonal line as before.

A Log Cabin block

It is possible to piece Log Cabin blocks together without the foundation square. Just cut the centre squares and strips as for the foundation method and, starting with the centre and strip A, place right sides together and stitch, taking the usual 0.75-cm (¼-in) seam allowance. Press the strip away from the centre, then continue adding the strips in the correct light and dark sequence. If several identical blocks are required, use this quick piecing method.

2 Sew all of the centre squares to strip A as indicated, leaving a small gap between each one.

Front

3 Trim the strips to size and press each.

Front

1 Cut the required number of strips and squares from your chosen fabric.

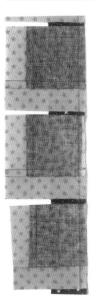

4 Join these units to strip B in the same way as shown.

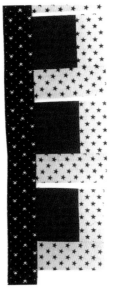

Front

5 Continue, keeping light and dark coloured fabrics in the correct sequence.

Front

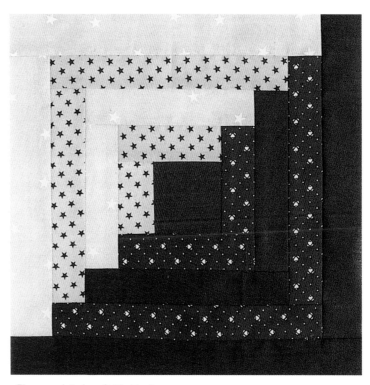

The complete Log Cabin block uses contrasting areas of light and dark colour to make dramatic impact.

Seminole Patchwork

The Seminole Indians of Florida devised this ingenious form of patchwork in the late 19th century, when trading with white settlers made hand-cranked sewing machines available. Long strips of fabric are first stitched together then cut and reassembled into dozens of different designs. Plain, bright colours are the most effective, providing contrast between the characteristic small geometric shapes. The resulting strips of patchwork were used to decorate clothing, household textiles or even dolls.

Measurements can be scaled up or down as long as the ratio remains the same. Approximately one third of the cut width of the strips is lost when the finished design is pieced. Designs can be reversed, offset or angled to give different effects.

Basically, strips are cut across the full width of the fabric. If using scissors, measure and mark the line to cut on for accuracy. The rotary cutting set is an ideal way of cutting the strips quickly and accurately.

When stitching the strips together use a shorter than normal stitch on your sewing machine to prevent the seam from coming undone when the seamed strips are cut into sections. Take 0.75 cm (¼ in) seam allowance. Avoid pleats on the front by gently pressing strips apart with your fingers as you iron the seam allowance to one side.

Simple reversed designs using two colours

1 Cut two strips in contrasting colours, one 2.5 cm (1 in) wide and the other 4.5 cm (1¾ in) wide. Sew the two strips right sides together, taking 0.75 cm (¼ in) of seam allowance.

2 Press the seam to one side on the back, then press the right side. Cut into 2.5-cm (1-in) sections across the strips.

3 Reverse alternate sections as shown.

4 Stitch the sections together in this sequence.

3 Reverse alternate sections and stitch back together, aligning the corners of the narrow strip as above.

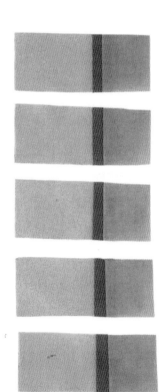

Reversed design using three colours

1 Cut three strips in the following widths: 4 cm (1½ in), 2 cm (¾ in), and 5.5 cm (2¼ in) and seam together.

2 Cut across the strips in sections 4 cm (1½ in) wide.

4 Trim away the excess fabric at the sides, as shown.

Offset design using two colours

Work across the width of the fabric so you have 112-cm (44-in) lengths. One strip should be dark and one strip light.

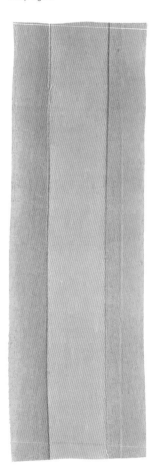

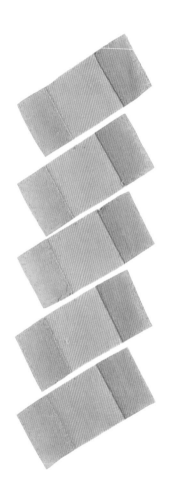

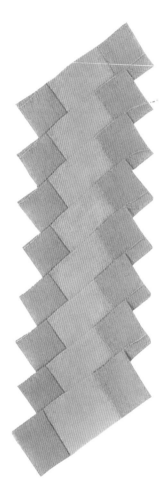

1 In the dark fabric, cut two strips 2.5 cm (1 in) wide. In the light fabric, cut one strip 4.5 cm (1¾ in) wide. Taking 0.75 cm (¼ in) of seam allowance, stitch the strips together as shown. Press the seams to one side.

2 Cut across the strips in 3-cm (1¼-in) pieces. Mark a dot at the top of the light strip, positioned 3 cm (1¼ in) in from the left hand seam. Place the cut pieces right sides together with the left-hand seam against the dot. This will offset each piece by 1.25 cm (½ in).

3 Continue to stitch the pieces together until enough length is created. Be careful to maintain accuracy when matching the dot to the seam.

4 Trim away the points at the sides, remembering to leave 0.75 cm (¼ in) of seam allowance beyond the points for joining, either to a plain strip or to another section of Seminole patchwork.

Offset design using three colours

Cut two strips of fabric A, 4 cm (1½ in) wide. Cut two strips of fabric B, 3 cm (1¼ in) wide.

Cut one strip of fabric C, 3 cm (1¼ in) wide.

1 Stitch the strips together in the sequence illustrated. Press seams to one side.

2 Cut into 3-cm (1¼ -in) sections across the seams.

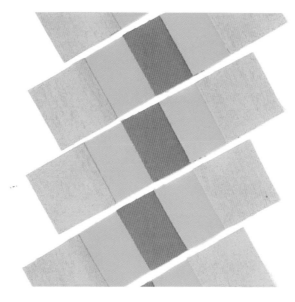

3 Reposition the pieces so that the corners of fabric C will match up.

4 Stitch the pieces together and press seams to one side.

5 Trim away the points at the sides of the length, leaving 0.75 cm (¼ in) beyond the corners of fabric A for seam allowance.

Angled design using two colours

1 Cut two colours of fabric into different widths as follows: fabric A – two strips of 4 cm (1½ in), fabric B – one strip of 2 cm (¾ in). Seam together as illustrated. Straighten one short end, then measure 75 cm (3 in) along from the top edge and cut at a slant.

A B A

2 Cut 5-cm (2-in) sections along the strip parallel with the angled edge that you cut in step one.

3 Seam these back together. Align the strips as shown, offsetting each narrow strip by 1.25 cm (½ in).

4 Press the seams and trim away the triangles at the sides, remembering to leave 0.75 cm (¼ in) of seam allowance.

The designs above and below are made by combining different strip sequences or a set of strips with a plain colour.

String Patchwork

This method of patchwork was devised to use up long strips of fabric – perhaps offcuts from dressmaking projects – which seem too narrow to be of any use at all. Seamed together and pressed flat, the strips result in pieces of patchwork that can be used as a single fabric to cut out the patches used to make up blocks. Choose a pattern which is simple to construct and decide which of the pieces in the block are to be made of the 'string' fabric. If necessary make templates. Many of the simpler blocks can be cut out without using templates. Before you begin, sort the fabrics to be used and wash and press them. Fraying can be minimised by placing the pieces in a net bag.

Making a string patchwork block

1 Cut strips of the same length in random widths between 2.5 and 7.5 cm (1 and 3 in).

If necessary strips can be joined to increase lengths to that of the longest piece. Don't try to keep the strips of a consistent width; triangular or wedge-shaped pieces give finished blocks an interesting effect of movement.

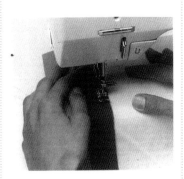

2 Machine-sew the strips together on the sewing machine using a smaller stitch than normal to prevent seams from coming undone when patches are cut.

Press seams to one side on the back and make sure that there are no small pleats between the seams by pressing again on the right side. If necessary, stitch strips to a foundation to stabilise flimsy fabrics.

3 Place strip the first strip right side up, aligning raw edges with those of the foundation fabric. Then position the subsequent strips face down against the preceding strip and stitch through the three layers, (two strips and the foundation) taking 0.75 cm (¼ in) of seam allowance. Flip the strip over to reveal the right side and press against the foundation. Continue until the foundation fabric is covered.

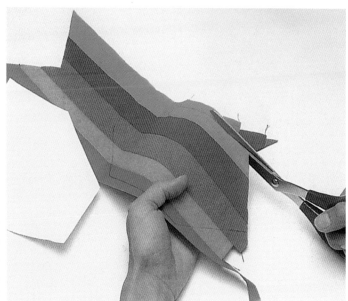

4 When you have created enough width to accommodate the template for your chosen block, cut out the patches and stitch the block together on the sewing machine.

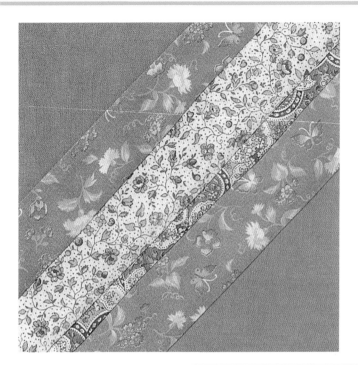

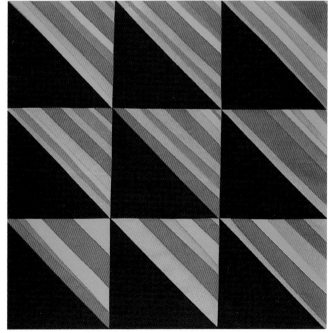

INDIAN HATCHET

This single patch from the Indian Hatchet design is set on a light background. It shows how different colours can create a totally different visual effect to the eight-block design opposite.

THIS ROMAN STRIPE DESIGN (left)
INDIAN HATCHET (above right)

Both these examples use solid black to complement the 'string' fabric.

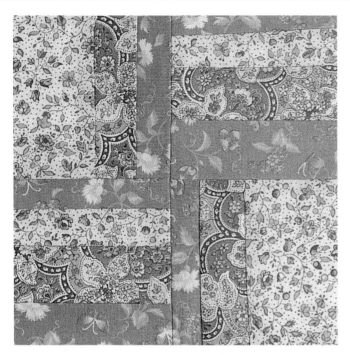

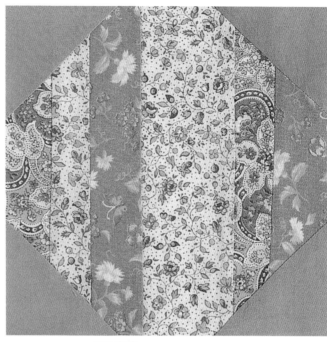

BASKET WEAVE (above left)
SNOWBALL (above right)
Both these blocks are attractive
examples of 'string' patchwork.

RAILFENCE

The Railfence block is very
easy to piece and is similar in
construction to the Basket
Weave block.

Special Effects

Piping

Wave Panel and Prairie Points

Suffolk Puffs

Biscuit Patchwork

Folded Star Patchwork

Cathedral Window

Crazy Patchwork

English Patchwork

If you want to add interest to the surface of a quilt there are various ways of creating texture by using three-dimensional sewing techniques or by fabric manipulation.

Piping is one design feature often used to highlight or to define particular areas of a quilt. It is especially interesting in pictorial quilts, where it can give depth and texture to a scene. Wave panels have a similar illustrative function and can be made from different widths of fabric. Other decorations, such as Suffolk Puffs and Prairie Points, also provide attractive and unusual additions to a quilt.

There are many varied and imaginative patchwork techniques which can be selected for an individual quilt, cushion or bed cover. Several of these, such as Biscuit, English and Folded Star patchwork, are illustrated on the following pages.

Three-dimensional effects with fabric

The pliable nature of fabric makes it an ideal medium to create surface texture. By pleating, tucking or inserting additional details between seams, an extra dimension can be added to the surface of a quilt, making it worthy of close examination. These techniques, sometimes referred to as 'fabric manipulation', can be used to provide focus areas or to emphasize the border in a geometric quilt. In pictorial quilts, a realistic appearance can be achieved to details by the use of special effects: try the wave panel to depict fields in a landscape, or prairie points as roof tiles in a house picture or the feathers on a bird.

Piping

Perhaps more familiar as a trim for upholstery and soft furnishings, piping can also be used very effectively in patchwork projects. As a finishing detail, for example on the edges of cushions, it can also add individuality to any project. Fabric areas can be separated with a line of piping in a contrasting colour, or it can be used as an additional frame around single blocks or the entire quilt, giving a crisp defining line. Piping is often used to outline individual features such as doorways, garden arches or fields to place emphasis on chosen areas.

DAPHNE RAMSEY
CATHEDRAL WINDOW WALL HANGING

This quilt combines a variation on the Cathedral Window technique and machine-embroidered crazy patchwork.

1 The most defined piping can be made by using piping cord. The piping itself should be cut into strips of 2.5 cm (1 in) or wider, and folded in half to enclose the cord. The piping and cord should then be seamed into the separate fabric areas as shown.

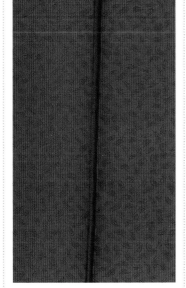

2 When the material is opened out, the cord within the piping is clearly defined.

3 Alternatively, simply sew the folded strip of piping into the seam and stitch, using a 0.75-cm (¼-in) seam allowance.

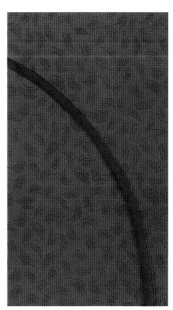

4 Curved piping can be produced by cutting bias strips (see page 109) to create the effect shown above.

Wave Panel and Prairie Points

The effect achieved by this technique belies its simplicity of construction. Folded strips of fabric are inserted between seams in the background, then stitched up and down in opposing directions to give the 'wave' effect. A dark/light contrast between background and folded strips gives a pleasing result which could be used as the centre panel for a cushion or bag. Toning colours might be used, for instance a combination of greens, to create realistic areas such as a ploughed field in a pictorial quilt. Experiment with different widths for both the backing and folded strips; a very narrow series of strips will appear flatter, while wider ones will stand away from the background, giving a more three-dimensional effect.

1 The tucks are cut and folded lengthwise, before being inserted and stitched into the seams with which the background strips are joined. Cut the 'tuck' fabric marginally narrower than the background strips, e.g. for background strips of 3 cm (1¼ in), cut tucks 2.5 cm (1 in) wide. Fold the tucks in half lengthwise, right sides together, and press.

2 Place the long edges of the background strips right sides together with the tucks between them. Seam the background strips together, trapping the tucks in the 0.75-cm (¼-in) seam allowance so that all four raw edges are together.

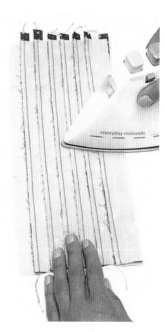

3 Press all the seams on the back in the same direction.

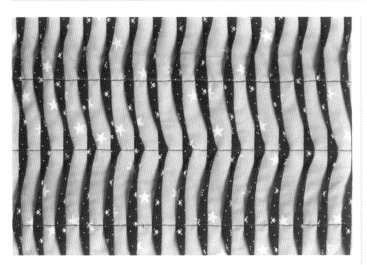

Prairie points

These small folded triangles can be used to add accent, colour or surface interest.

4 On the right side stitch the tucks against the background down the centre of the panel, then press them in the opposite direction on each side of the line and stitch down to the background again to create the wave effect.

Continue to stitch the tucks up and down until the whole panel is completed.

1 Fold a square of fabric in half to create a rectangle, then fold the corners across to make the triangle.

All raw edges will now be together on the longest side of the triangle. Press well to form sharp creases.

Alternatives

1 A similar effect can be created by stitching pin tucks into the fabric rather than inserting the tucks. There will be no dark/light contrast, only the effect of shadow created by the way light falls on the fabric.

2 Pinch the pin tucks together at regular alternating intervals for a 'smocked' effect.

2 Insert the resulting triangle between two pieces of fabric in the seam allowance (so that all raw edges are together). Stitch, trapping the triangle in the seam.

3 In this panel prairie points are trapped between wedge-shaped strips of fabric. The double border has a folded strip of piping inserted between the two strips to add a narrow, contrasting line.

Suffolk Puffs

Also known as yo-yo, this technique was used to make light bed throws from scrap fabrics in the 1920s and '30s. Circles of fabric are gathered and the thread is pulled up tightly to create medallion shapes. These are caught together at a point on each side, leaving spaces between which give a decorative, lace-like effect. The best fabric to use is fine lightweight cotton with a close weave that does not easily fray and will allow the gathering thread to be pulled up tightly.

1 Decide on the size of the finished yo-yo unit and cut a circle of fabric twice this size. A piece 11.5 cm (4½ in) in diameter will give a finished unit of 5.7 cm (2¼ in).

2 Turn a narrow single hem on the cut circle of fabric. An easy way to make an even hem on the fabric is to tack it over a circle of paper, turning the seam allowance over the paper in the same way as for English patchwork. Press the fabric circle with the paper inside it, then remove the tacking and paper. The turning will be firmly and evenly creased, and the circle will be the size of the paper shape.

WHIP STITCH

Whip stitch, also called oversewing, is used instead of slipstitch to join two folded edges of fabric when a strong joining is needed. It is an ideal stitch for joining the circles together, see step 5 right.

3 Using thread to match the fabric, doubled if necessary to take the strain of pulling up the gathers, work a ring of running stitches round the outer edges of the circle. Leave a long knotted end at the beginning of the work.

4 When the circle of stitches is complete, pull the thread tightly from both ends to gather up the fabric. Make the opening as small as possible by pulling the gathers closely. Knot the thread ends together and stitch them out of sight. Flatten the fabric circle with the opening in the centre and steam press. Make as many units as necessary for the project.

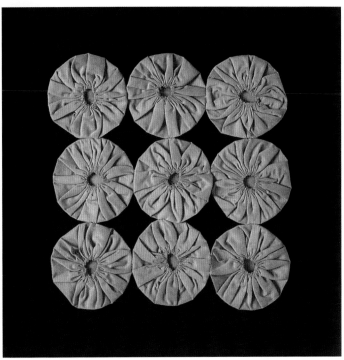

5 Join the units together with four or five whip stitches at a point on each side of the units, catching the folds together. Neaten the thread ends.

6 If a more solid appearance is required, the project can be mounted and appliquéd onto another fabric.

Biscuit Patchwork

This rather novel method of patchwork makes a very light, warm form of cot or bed cover. Patches in multiples of a single shape, usually squares, are made into pockets and filled with stuffing. These individual pouches are then sewn together to create a textured surface of raised squares separated by the joining channels. No quilting is necessary as the separate areas are complete units which hold the stuffing in place, preventing it from migrating. Designs for biscuit quilts can be adapted from any traditional designs which are made up of squares; Trip Around the World, Irish Chain or even a simple nine patch are all suitable. This would also be an ideal project for a scrap or charm quilt.

1 Each of the 'biscuits' is made by sewing a larger top square onto a base. Preshrunk cotton in a light colour is a suitable fabric for the base squares. Decide what size to make the unit and cut base squares to this measurement plus 1.5 cm (½ in) for seam allowances. Cut the top squares 2.5 to 3.5 cm (1 to 1½ in) larger than the base. A bigger difference in the size between the top square and the base will result in a fatter pouch and thus a thicker quilt overall.

2 Place the larger square on top of the base, wrong sides facing, and pin the corners together. Then pleat the sides of the top square evenly and stitch the two layers together on three sides by hand or machine.

Stitch inside the seam allowance so that these stitches will be cleverly concealed when the biscuit units are joined together.

3 Push loose stuffing into the open side of each piece, using the same amount for each square. Pin the opening and stitch the two layers together, pleating the top square in the same way as on the other three sides to enclose the stuffing.

  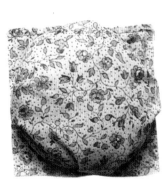

4 Make enough units to complete your project. Stitch them together by hand or machine taking 0.75 cm (¼ in) as seam allowance. Finger press the seams open or to one side on the back. They should not be ironed as this may damage the stuffing.

5 To conceal the seams on the back, line the completed biscuit top with a piece of harmonizing fabric, finishing the edges with binding or by turning the edges together (see page 108). The quilt top and backing fabric can be secured together with stitches or knots at regular intervals between the biscuit units.

Folded Star Patchwork

Rectangles of fabric folded into small triangles make these crisp star medallions, which can be incorporated into quilts or used as centres for cushions and smaller items. When selecting fabric for Folded Star, look for pure cotton which creases well, and choose a colour scheme with sharp contrasts. Plain colours or small prints are the most effective; larger prints will not work as well when folded into small units. The medallions are worked from the centre – each round of triangles held down at the point and stitched to a foundation square. The folding and overlapping produces quite a thickness of fabric, so it is not practical to quilt it.

1 Cut a square of foundation fabric larger than the finished size of the medallion by about 5 cm (2 in) all round. To make the triangles cut a strip of fabric 4 cm (1½ in) wide across the fabric from selvedge to selvedge. Fold down a 0.75-cm (¼-in) hem along one long edge. Cut this strip into 6.5-cm (2½-in) pieces.
Fold these pieces in half to find the centre, then fold the corners down to create triangles and steam press.

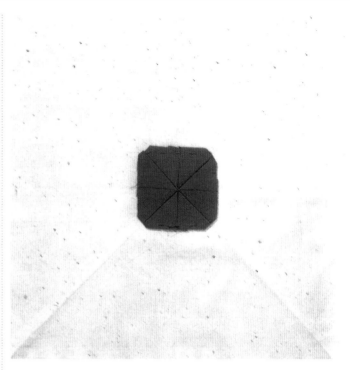

2 Round 1: press the foundation fabric to form creases vertically, horizontally and diagonally and arrange the first four triangles, folded sides on top, in the centre with the points just touching. The angled sides should be in line with the diagonal creases. Secure the points to the foundation fabric with a stitch, and tack or, if the fabric frays easily, use overcasting round the outer edge of the triangles. Trim off the corners to reduce bulk.

OVERCASTING
Overcasting is used to finish the edges of fabrics that fray easily. Work from either direction, taking the thread over the edge of the fabric. Do not pull the thread too tightly, or the edges of the fabric will curl and make bulges.

5 Round 4: make sixteen triangles. Position eight of these 1.25 cm (½ in) back from the points of round 3, then place the other eight with points just touching the star points of round 2. Stitch down the points and round the outer edges as before. Trim away the triangle corners.

Further rounds require sixteen triangles. Continue to build the star outwards, setting the triangles back by 1.25 cm (½ in) on each round until the star is the desired size.

3 Round 2: with contrasting fabric make eight triangles. Position the points 1.25 cm (½ in) away from the centre and stitch to the foundation through the triangles on round 1, catching the points down with a stitch and tacking round the outer edges. Trim the corners.

4 Round 3: make eight triangles to contrast with the previous round and position these 1.25 cm (½ in) back from the points of round 2. Stitch down the points and tack round the outer edges as before. Trim the corners.

FRAMING THE STAR
To set the star into a circular frame cut two pieces of fabric to the correct size, plus seam allowances. One is for the frame and one for a facing. For a 25.4-cm (10-in) square frame cut two 26.7-cm (10½-in) squares. Press and pin them right sides together. Measure the circle for the 'window' and mark this in the centre of the squares. Stitch round the circle, then cut out the centre leaving 0.75 cm (¼ in) of seam allowance. Clip all round the seam allowance just short of the stitching line, then turn the facing to the inside and press. The two fabrics are now right sides out. Position the frame over the medallion, pin and stitch round the circle. Trim the square to size and tack the three layers together. The bottom layer is the calico backing of the star.

Cathedral Window

This technique uses squares of folded fabric as a background to show off small 'windows' of decorative fabric. The preparation of the background squares reduces them in size by just over half, so allow about 2¼ times the finished size of the foundation fabric. The size of the squares is flexible, but 15 or 18 cm (6 or 7 in), which results in a window about 5 cm (2 in) square, is a popular size. Experiment with different fabrics – a striped background fabric gives an interesting effect. Windows can be made with floral or shiny fabric. You could also contrast a patterned background with plain inserts.

Prepare the foundation squares by hand or machine.

By hand

1 Cut a square of foundation fabric and turn a small single hem [about 0.75 cm (¼ in)] all round. Press flat.
Fold the corners to the centre, pin down and press well to give a sharp crease.

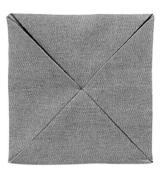

2 Repeat step 1, folding corners to the centre, then fasten these down through all layers with one or two small cross stitches.

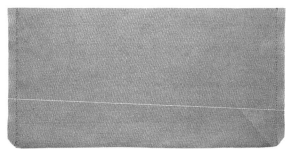

By machine

1 Cut the square of foundation fabric, fold in half and press. Stitch up the two short sides taking a 0.75 cm (¼ in) seam allowance. Clip the corners off the seams on the folded side and press seams open.

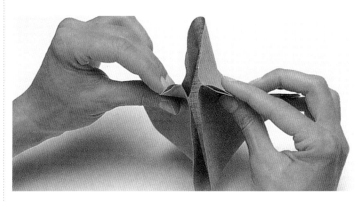

2 Pull the open edge apart so that the two seam ends meet.

3 Stitch across this opening, leaving a gap to turn the square through to the right side.

4 Clip the corners off this seam at each end and press seams open. Turn through the gap right side out, poke out the corners and press.

5 Fold the corners to the centre and secure through all layers with cross stitches as for the hand-stitched method.

Joining the squares
Whichever way you have prepared the squares, the procedure is the same from now on.

1 When you have prepared enough foundation squares, place them right sides together. Join along one edge with whip stitch from corner to corner.

2 Join as many squares as you need for your design into a block. As squares are joined, the area into which the 'window' will be stitched is created. This is a square of the decorative fabric set as a diamond 'on point'. Measure the area and cut squares of decorative fabric for inserts. Place them in position as shown, over the join of two squares, and pin.

3 Curl the folded edges of the stitched squares over the decorative insert, then hem down in a smooth curve over each side, using thread that matches the foundation fabric.

4 Repeat until all the window spaces are filled. To fill the triangular shapes at the edges, fold the decorative squares in half diagonally and pin them in position. Then hem the two curved edges down and slipstitch the folds together along the outer edge.

CATHEDRAL WINDOW

Crazy Patchwork

The crazy block uses shapes which fit together in an irregular but economical way. The jigsaw-like construction allows for the use of every available scrap of fabric, wasting none of what was once a valuable resource.

By the last quarter of the 19th century the crazy quilt was transformed into a 'throw' made of rich fabrics such as silk, velvet and taffeta, and often embellished with sentimental mementoes, lavish embroidery, lace and ribbons. The only similarity between these Victorian crazy quilts and their earlier predecessors was their randomly cut shapes.

Crazy quilt patches are stitched onto squares of foundation fabric so no wadding is necessary. There are various ways of constructing a block.

Starting in a corner

1 Start with a foundation square of white sheeting or similar weight fabric which measures 25 to 35 cm (10 to 14 in) square. Position the first patch in one corner and pin it down securely.

2 Work across from the corner, pinning down further pieces and overlapping the edges by about 0.75 to 1.25 cm (¼ to ½ in) to fit them together like a jigsaw.

3 When the foundation square is covered, turn under the overlapping raw edges and tack down the pieces to the foundation. Leave raw edges around the outside of the square – these will be contained by the seams when the blocks are joined together.

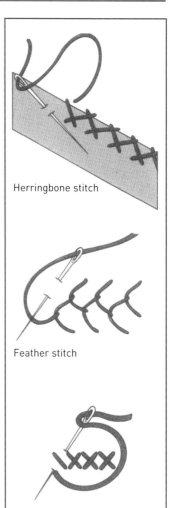

Herringbone stitch

Feather stitch

Cross stitch

In crazy patchwork, linear stitches such as herringbone, feather and cross stitch form attractive decoration to the seams. They also hold the patches down securely.

4 Embroider over the edges where the patches overlap and meet. Ribbons, lace, fragments of embroidery and old buttons or beads. can be applied to the patches.

Trim the completed squares to the same size and join them together with a 0.75-cm (¼ -in) seam allowance, stitching through all layers. If preferred, the blocks can be separated by sashing strips.

Starting with a centre patch

In this method the block is built outward, around a centre patch. Prepare the foundation square as for method 1 and select a piece of interesting fabric for the centre patch.

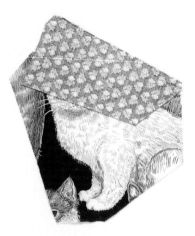

1 Cut out a four- or five-sided shape, and put this right side up in the centre on top of the foundation. Press lightly and pin down.

2 Select a second fabric and cut a random straight-sided piece. Place this right side down, aligning one straight edge against one side of the first patch. Stitch by hand or machine through the two layers and the foundation fabric using a running stitch and taking 0.75 cm (¼ in) of seam allowance.

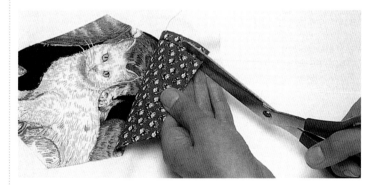

3 Flip patch 2 over to reveal the right side of the fabric and trim so that the straight edges of patch 1 extend along the edges of patch 2.

4 Add further patches right side down along the straight edges created as you stitch and flip them over.

5 Continue until the foundation square is completely covered. Trim the square and press.

6 The blocks can be joined edge to edge as illustrated here in Cat Crazy, or separated with sashing strips. This quilt is machine quilted.

English Patchwork

Sometimes called 'mosaic' or 'paper' patchwork, each patch is shaped by tacking the fabric onto a paper template. The pieces are sewn together by hand using a tiny overcast or whip stitch. Although this method of patchwork is time-consuming, it has the advantage of accuracy when used to sew together intricate interlocking shapes like hexagons, diamonds and triangles. As soon as a patch is surrounded by others, the paper can be removed and then used again.

To design a mosaic patchwork, use isometric or squared graph paper. You can use any shape or combination of shapes which fit together without leaving gaps. Templates can be cut from graph paper and glued onto stiff card, or you can use commercially available ones. Window templates enable you to frame a particular part of the fabric (see page 13).

1 To make the papers, draw around the template onto a good quality cartridge paper – if the paper is too thin it will bend easily. Cutting the papers accurately is important, so cut each one individually. Cut out enough papers to start your project.

2 Pin a paper to the wrong side of the fabric and cut out the patch, adding 0.75-cm (¼-in) seam allowance as you cut the fabric. Pin the paper to the fabric with the fabric grain running the same way throughout. (If you want to use the fabric design in a particular way, such as stripes forming a ring, disregard this rule.)

3 Start with a knot and tack the backing paper to the fabric, folding over the seam allowance. Be sure that the edge of the paper goes right into the fold. At the corners fold the fabric over and secure with a stitch. Finish with a backstitch. Some shapes, like diamonds and triangles, have an acute angle. To reduce bulk, trim the sharp corner off the fabric. If a tab of fabric projects beyond the sharp points, manoeuvre it to the back when stitching the patches together.

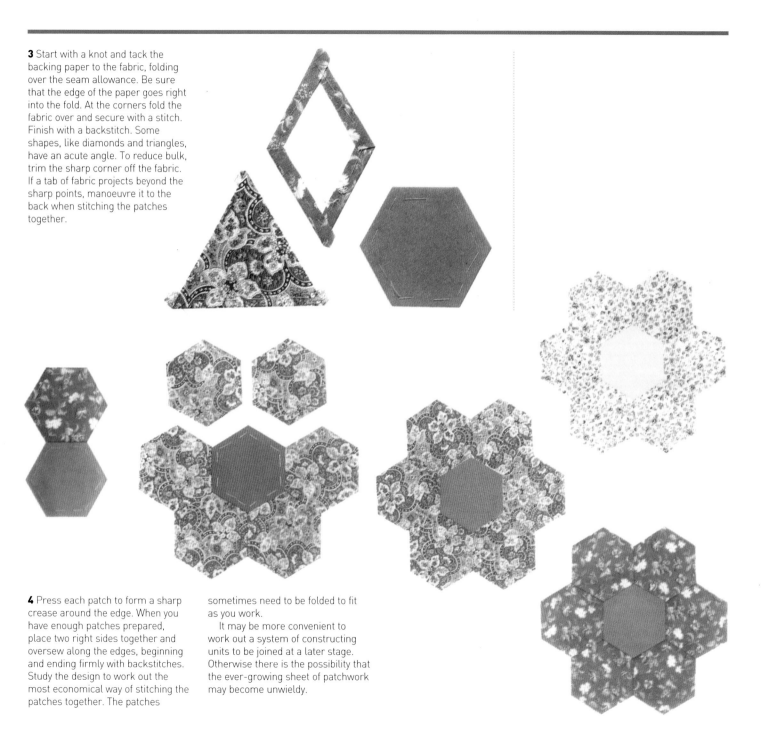

4 Press each patch to form a sharp crease around the edge. When you have enough patches prepared, place two right sides together and oversew along the edges, beginning and ending firmly with backstitches. Study the design to work out the most economical way of stitching the patches together. The patches sometimes need to be folded to fit as you work.

It may be more convenient to work out a system of constructing units to be joined at a later stage. Otherwise there is the possibility that the ever-growing sheet of patchwork may become unwieldy.

Appliqué

In the technique of appliqué, pieces of fabric are cut out and stitched onto a foundation. Originally developed as a means of extending the life of a garment or bedspread, or of making expensive materials go further, its potential as a medium for decorative and pictorial designs in fabric was soon realised and exploited. Because curved shapes can be more easily used than in pieced patchwork, elaborate designs using motifs such as flowers, birds and fruit became a way of showing off the skills of needlewomen in the 19th century. Baltimore brides' quilts, made of elaborately appliquéd blocks containing floral and patriotic elements, are fine examples of this technique.

KATHARINE GUERRIER
FRUIT BASKET BLOCK
This block combines patchwork and machine-appliqué techniques. Final details are added with machine embroidery.

Designing for Hand Appliqué

When the separate pieces of an appliqué design are stitched down by hand, the raw edges of the fabrics must be turned under, before being hemmed to the foundation to prevent fraying. When designing for hand appliqué , bear this in mind and try to strike a balance between shapes which are so simple that they look crude, and those which have such elaborate curves that difficulties may occur in stitching down the edges. Sketch out a few ideas using the outline shapes of leaves, petals or fruit. Appliqué can be used to create one large single image such as the Tree of Life designs, but for a first project try a smaller panel which may be the beginning of a repeat block quilt or could be made into a cushion.

Hand appliqué

1 When you are satisfied with your design, decide on the number of templates required and trace each shape from the drawing.

2 From the traced shapes make full-size templates from thin card.

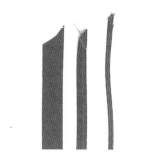

3 Cut a piece of foundation fabric allowing 5 cm (2 in) extra or so all round for turnings. Using the templates to draw each shape, copy the design onto the foundation fabric. It may be advisable to use a fabric marker which can be erased, in case your appliqué shapes do not quite cover the lines.

MAKING BIAS STRIPS

To achieve a consistent width which lies flat and will curve smoothly, make a bias tube which cuts out the need to turn under a seam allowance as you stitch. A 25- to 28-cm (10- to 11-in) square of fabric will make enough strips to make stems for one block. Begin with a true bias by folding the fabric diagonally making a 45-degree angle. Press a crease on the fold line and cut along this crease. From the resulting triangle cut 2.5-cm (1-in) wide bias strips. Fold a strip in half lengthwise wrong sides together. With the folded edge next to the presser foot of your sewing machine stitch a narrow tube. Trim away excess seam allowance. Roll the tube so that the seam lies down the centre and press flat. A bias press bar will make this process easier. This is a narrow, flat piece of metal or heat-resistant nylon which can be pushed into the tube, making it easier to manoeuvre the seam to the flat of the bar and press it with a hot iron. Remove the bar and press again. If your design calls for narrower stems than can be made using this method, cut bias strips 1.25 or 2 cm (½ or ¾ in) wide, then overlap one long edge over the other one, making a narrow strip. Tack the edges to hold them in place, making sure the width of the strip is consistent.

4 To make stems and vines (which are often the first pieces to be stitched down) make bias strips as described. Place the stems in position on the foundation, then pin and stitch them in place, concealing the seam or the fold at the back.

5 Select suitable fabrics for each shape and mark round the templates, placing these right side up on the right side of the fabric. This marked line indicates where the fabric is to be turned under.

Mark and cut out the patch, allowing up to 0.75 cm (¼ in) for turning, clip concave curves within the turning (no more than 3 mm (⅛ in)), then fold under the raw edges on the line marked round the template.

6 The clipped concave curves will fan out as they are turned under. Fabric may have to be folded twice on sharp points in order to reduce bulk, so trim away as much as you can from the point without cutting too close to the drawn line.

7 For inside points, clip into the point and fold under the turning, being careful not to allow fraying at the inner point. Tack to hold the turnings in place until the piece is stitched to the foundation.

Building up the design

1 Many appliqué patterns have shapes which overlap. Begin with the shapes which lie partially underneath. The raw edges which will be covered do not need to be turned under. Build up the design using a logical sequence to stitch down the shapes. Where several layers are stitched down on top of each other, cut away the foundation fabric from behind, 0.75 cm (¼ in) in from the stitching line to reduce bulk. Press appliqué on a thick pad such as a towel to prevent it from being flattened.

2 Embroidered details can be added when the design is complete. Assemble the appliqué block or quilt top with the wadding and backing, and quilt the background and around the appliqué shapes.

HEMMING STITCH

Using a single strand of thread to match the patch, sew the shapes to the background with a neat hemming stitch. Make sure that the needle goes straight down from the fold of the fabric into the background and comes up about 0.75 cm (¼ in) further along into the fold. For a more visible, decorative stitch, appliqué can be stitched down with a small running stitch. There is a special needle, designed to help make small, neat stitches, that has been developed for appliqué work .

USING FREEZER PAPER

For each fabric shape cut out a corresponding piece of freezer paper. Place this paper on the wrong side of the patch with the waxed side of the paper uppermost. Clip curves, then fold over the turning onto the waxed side of the paper (above left). Press down the turnings with a dry iron. The fabric will stick to and be shaped by the paper (above right). Stitch the patch in position. To remove the paper leave a gap to detach it gently and pull it through before closing the seam, or cut away the foundation from behind the patch 0.75 cm (¼ in) from the stitching line and pull it out from the back.

Appliqué shapes can also be formed by tacking them onto papers cut to the shape of the desired patch, then pressing them to form a crease round the outer edge. Remove the tacking stitches and the paper before sewing the shape down.

Machine Appliqué

If you have a sewing machine which will form an even, close satin stitch – the same stitch that is used for buttonholes – then you will be able to work appliqué panels by machine. The satin stitch is used to stitch down the shapes and cover the raw edges simultaneously, so no seam allowances are necessary. When designing panels for machine appliqué, begin with simple shapes which can be easily guided through the sewing machine without too many sharp turns. Flowers, fruit and leaf shapes can provide inspiration when designing appliqué panels. Sketch out a few ideas before starting to cut fabric.

1 When you have worked out a design decide whether it is necessary to make templates; simple shapes may be cut freehand. Trace more complicated shapes from your drawing and make templates from thin card.

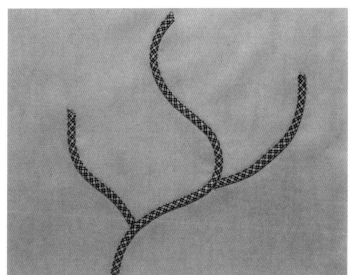

2 Cut a piece of fabric for the background slightly larger than the desired finished size and begin by stitching the preliminary details such as stems (see step 4, page 86) using machine straight stitch. If you are adding appliqué to a patchwork block, you should assemble the patchwork block first.

3 Choose fabrics appropriate to your design and press well to remove all creases. When stitching appliqué shapes by machine, the background has a tendency to pucker. To avoid this use a fusible fabric adhesive which is bonded onto a paper backing. Place this against the wrong side of the appliqué fabric with the glue side, which feels slightly rougher than the paper side, down. Iron to the fabric with a medium heat.

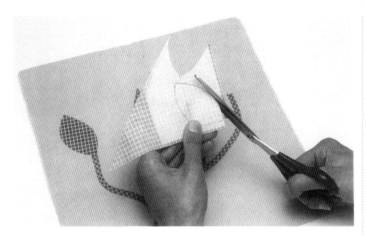

4 Appliqué shapes can be drawn on paper freehand or you can draw around templates made from your design. Cut out the appliqué shapes and the paper together, then peel away the paper.

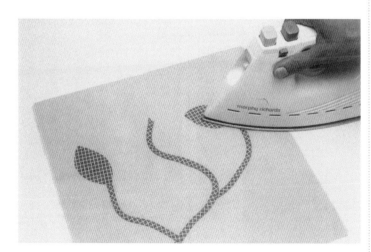

5 Position the appliqué shape onto the background and press with a medium iron to fuse. The use of fusible fabric adhesive will slightly stiffen the fabric. If you want your panel to remain soft, cut out the appliqué from fabric, place it in position on the background and tack it down.

6 When all the appliqué shapes are in position, set the machine to the correct stitch. If you are not using fusible fabric adhesive, stitch round the appliqué shape first with a straight stitch or open zigzag stitch to hold it, then set the stitch to a close satin stitch. Loosen the top tension slightly if you can to prevent the bottom thread from showing on the top. Guide the shapes through the machine, turning to follow the curves. If you can, vary the width of the zigzag as you go. Try narrowing it to a point for leaf tips, or widen it to make more rounded curves. Variegated machine embroidery threads will give an interesting effect round the edges of the appliqué shapes.

7 Extra machine-stitched details, such as on the edges of the leaves can be added.

Reverse Appliqué

Reverse appliqué is done by placing two or more layers of fabric together and then cutting away upper layers in a design. When it is worked by hand, the raw edges of the fabric must be turned under to neaten them. Choose finely woven, pure cotton fabrics that will not easily fray for reverse appliqué; when turning the fabric under in curves and sharp inner corners, the fabric has to be clipped and this may create a weak point at which a coarsely woven fabric will fray.

The same principles apply to reverse appliqué by machine or by hand: fabric is layered and stitched together and the upper layers are cut away to reveal the design. The difference is that no turnings need to be made when sewing by machine, as the shapes are stitched together with a close satin stitch which holds down the fabrics and seals the raw edges simultaneously.

Hand reverse appliqué

1 Cut two pieces of fabric in the desired finished size of the work, allowing 2.5 cm (1 in) or so extra around the outer edge for turnings. Press them together, placing the right side of the lower fabric against the wrong side of the upper one. Draw the design onto the top fabric, then tack all round the outer edge of it, just over 1.25 cm (½ in) away.

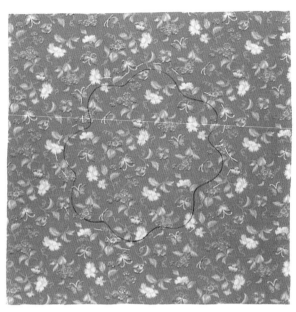

2 Using a small, sharp pair of scissors, cut away the top 0.75 cm (¼ in) inside the drawn line. Clip any concave curves and inner corners towards, and just inside, the drawn line.

3 Select thread which matches the top fabric. Turning under the raw edges on the drawn line as you go, slipstitch the top layer of fabric to the one underneath. Use small, neat stitches and turn the edge under with the point of your needle, holding it in place with your thumb just ahead of your stitching. At sharp inner corners, place two or three stitches close together to prevent fraying.

4 The edges of the two layers of fabric can be tacked together around the outside of the piece, or excess fabric from the top layer could be trimmed away 0.75 cm (¼ in) from your stitching if preferred. This will reduce bulk on the finished piece.

5 For a third colour, draw a second shape onto the appliqué fabric. Cut the third fabric slightly larger than this shape and pin it behind the drawing on the front. Tack round the drawing as in step 1, then cut away the new shape and hem down. Use thread to match the second colour.

6 More shapes can be added, building up the design with three or four colours. Press reverse appliqué on a thick pad such as a towel to prevent it from becoming too flattened.

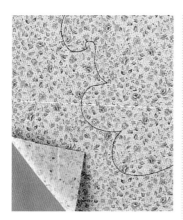

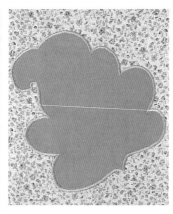

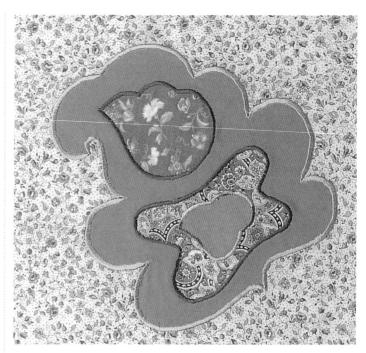

Machine reverse appliqué

1 Cut two squares of fabric in the desired size, remembering to allow extra fabric for turnings. Place them both right side up, one on top of the other, and steam press. Pin or tack them together. Draw the design to be appliquéd on the top fabric, then stitch round the drawn line with a straight stitch.

3 Set the machine to a close satin stitch (buttonhole stitch) and sew round the shape, covering the raw edges and stitching the top and bottom layers together.

Satin stitch has a tendency to pucker the fabric. To prevent this tack a piece of thin paper underneath the design to be stitched, which can be torn away afterwards.

5 The design can be built up by drawing further shapes on the area of the appliqué.

Cut pieces of fabric slightly larger than the area of the drawing and tack them to the back, behind the drawn shape. Straight stitch round the drawn line, then repeat steps 2 and 3. As you progress, trim away excess fabrics outside the stitching line on the back to reduce bulk.

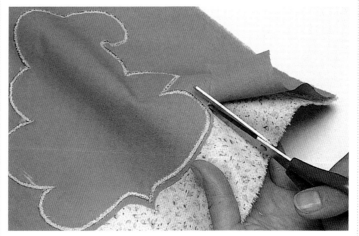

2 With a small, sharp pair of scissors, carefully cut away the top layer inside the line and close to the stitching, being careful not to cut the underneath layer as well.

4 Trim away the excess base fabric on the back, outside the area of the appliqué and about 0.75 cm (¼ in) away from the stitching line.

Mola appliqué

An elaborate form of reverse appliqué, molas are made by the Kuna Indians from the San Blas islands of Panama. Panels are made to decorate the front and back panels of the traditional blouses they call the 'mola', still largely worn as everyday clothing by the women and girls. When the government of Panama tried to prohibit the wearing of molas during an attempt to integrate the island populations, the move was met with resistance and molas continued to be worn as an expression of pride and independence. Designs worked on molas record plant and animal life, scenes from local ceremonies and religious lore, and even contemporary events. Up to four layers are worked in fine stitching with narrow channels, more colours being added by smaller pieces which are inserted in strategic positions. Final details are embroidered on.

PA NDAU CUSHION COVER
Pa Ndau designs and molas are becoming highly collectable.

ANN TUCK
CAYACCA
A three-layer mola quilt using traditional appliqué techniques. The design lines were worked by stitching through from the back of the basic fabric onto the middle layer which was then cut and hemmed down. The third layer was worked in the same way.

Pa Ndau

Pa Ndau is another form of complex reverse appliqué made by the Hmong hill tribes of south-east Asia. Geometric shapes abstracted from natural forms such as snails, spider's webs, stars and elephants have symbolic meanings and are worked on two or three layers of fabric. The resulting panels are used to decorate clothing and household textiles. As with molas, embroidery is used to embellish the designs.

Appliqué Perse

Appliqué Perse or Broderie Perse is a technique of cutting motifs from printed fabrics and rearranging them on a plain background before stitching them down. Originally a means of making rare and expensive fabrics go further, or preserving the life of a partly worn piece, it became very popular in England in the 18th century and later in America. Fabrics imported from India were block printed with flora and fauna and brightly coloured, sometimes by hand. Despite attempts by the British textile industry to ban the import of these fabrics, their popularity was such that designs were copied from English embroideries to cater to British tastes. Their scarcity, largely due to the law passed in 1721 banning their use on clothing or household furnishings, increased the popularity of Appliqué Perse as the technique could be used to make small amounts of the fabric go further. Appliqué Perse can be done in the traditional way – by hand – or the technique can be updated by using machine appliqué.

Choosing fabrics

When choosing suitable fabrics for Appliqué Perse, look for those with clearly defined motifs such as flowers, birds, animals, etc. Select those which can be cut out fairly simply. Fine stems and other small details are best added as surface embroidery later.

By hand

If working by hand, cut out the motifs allowing 0.75 to 1.5 cm (¼ to ½ in) extra for turnings. Prepare the pieces by turning under the raw edges using any of the methods described for hand appliqué (see pages 85–87). Arrange them on a plain background. Pin down and stitch as for hand appliqué. Add further details to the pieces with embroidery.

By machine

If sewing the motifs down by machine, cut them out with a narrow outline; remember that machine satin stitch takes up a width of about 3 mm (⅛ in). Arrange them onto the background and tack them down, then stitch round the edges with a close satin stitch. Try using decorative thread as an embellishment. Use machine embroidery to add fine details.

Shadow Appliqué

In this appliqué technique the patches which make up the design are trapped between two layers of fabric. A light coloured plain fabric such as cream or white cotton is best for the base. The top fabric must be transparent so that the design shows through: organza, chiffon or a close net would be suitable. The two layers are stitched together round each of the appliqué shapes with a running stitch which holds the design in position. No seam allowance is necessary as there are no turnings made on the appliqué.

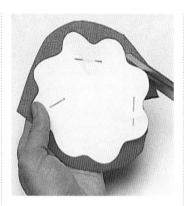

1 Cut out appliqué shapes according to your chosen design. Use strong, plain colours, as the sheer top layer gives the fabrics a muted effect. As with machine appliqué, if you are using fairly simple shapes, appliqués can be cut freehand. Whether or not you are using templates, do not add seam allowance. A light coating of spray starch will prevent the edges from fraying.

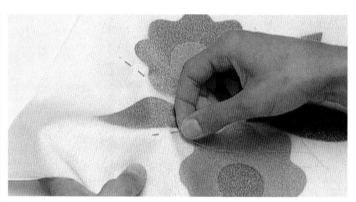

3 Smooth the sheer fabric over the top of the appliqués. Pin and tack the layers together around the design and the outer edges.

2 Arrange the design on the foundation fabric using a small dab of fabric glue to hold pieces in position.

4 Using thread which blends with the top layer of fabric, stitch round each of the appliqué shapes with running stitch. Details such as leaf veins and stems can be embroidered on top with a contrasting embroidery thread.

Hawaiian Appliqué

Patchwork and quilting were first introduced to the Hawaiian islanders by missionaries who started to go there in the early 19th century. A unique design style, consisting of a large appliqué called a Kapa Lau, which was stitched to the foundation fabric, developed. These were designed much in the same way that paper snowflakes are cut – the top fabric is folded and cut in layers. Shapes which inspired the designs were taken from everyday things such as flowers, leaves and fruit. Individual designs were jealously guarded; it was considered wrong to copy another person's design. Hawaiian quilts are traditionally made in two bright plain colours, usually red or blue on white. The appliqué covers most of the background, which can be as big as a full-size bedspread or as small as a cushion. The quilting, known as echo or wave quilting, follows the shape of the appliqué and radiates out in lines, rather like ripples, across the background to the edges of the piece. In Hawaii the quilting is called Luma Lau.

1 Try out folded paper designs before making a final choice. Fold paper squares in half, then into quarters and finally once more into eighths. Draw and cut the design between the two folded edges, which should remain uncut. Open out the paper and check the designs until you have a satisfactory one. Cut out a one-eighth segment to use as a template.

2 Cut two squares of fabric 5 cm (2 in) or so larger than the paper pattern, one for the background and one for the appliqué. Fold each one in half and in half again, ironing the creases and making sure the grain runs straight with the folds. Finally fold diagonally, pressing again. Pin the paper template onto the appliqué fabric and mark round the shape. Remove the paper and pin the fabric layers back together. Cut out the appliqué with a pair of sharp scissors, making sure that the layers do not shift.

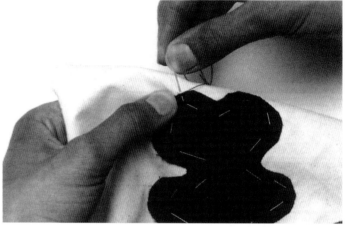

4 Starting near the centre and turning under the raw edges of the appliqué with the point of the needle as you go, slip-hem the appliqué shape using thread to match. When there is a sharp inner turn, make several stitches to prevent fraying. To stitch points, work up to the tip, then tuck under the fabric on the other side with the needle and continue. Always use small, close stitches.

3 Unfold the background fabric and smooth it out on a flat surface. Remove the pins from the appliqué, unfold it and position it onto the background, lining up the creases and pinning the two layers together. Work from the centre outwards and smooth as you go. Tack all round the shape 1 cm (⅜ in) from the edges.

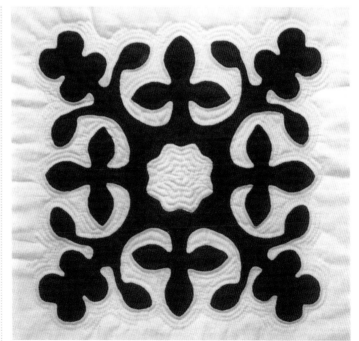

5 To quilt, assemble the top, wadding and backing and tack the three layers together. Quilt, echoing the shapes of the appliqué in lines about 1.25 cm (½ in) apart.

Stained Glass Appliqué

Stained glass appliqué is a relatively recent form, which uses bold shapes outlined with narrow black lines to resemble stained glass. The fabric pieces are cut out and arranged on a square of foundation fabric edge to edge, rather like the pieces of a jigsaw puzzle. The raw edges of the fabric shapes are then covered with bias strips which imitate the leading in a stained-glass window. When designing for this technique, use simple shapes with gentle curves. Each drawn line must either connect to another or go to the edge of the design just like in real stained glass. Avoid very small shapes – curving the bias strips which form the separating 'leading' is too difficult. For design ideas look at stylised drawings in children's books or large print fabrics and wallpapers with distinct linear designs. Wrought-iron railings, or even real stained-glass windows, can be a source of inspiration for the more ambitious needleworker.

1 On good quality cartridge paper, make a drawing at the full size of the completed panel. Trace the drawing, then on the other side of the tracing paper mark all the lines with an embroidery transfer pencil. For the foundation cut a piece of light coloured cotton or calico slightly larger than the finished size of the panel. Transfer the design onto the foundation fabric with a hot dry iron.

2 Number each shape on the drawing and the tracing, then cut up the drawing to use as templates. The numbered tracing is your guide to the design. Do not add any seam allowances.

3 Use the templates to cut out fabric shapes. Tack them onto the foundation around the edges of each shape, placing the shapes edge to edge on the transferred design.

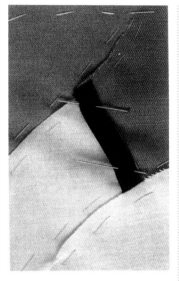

5 Place the bias strips along the edges of the shapes, centring it so that all raw edges are covered. Pin in place carefully

6 Study the design to decide which strips to apply first – those which run into a continuing line must be tucked under and stitched down.

4 When the foundation fabric is covered and all appliqué shapes are tacked down, make bias strips (see page 85). A 45-cm (18-in) square of black fabric was enough for the illustrated Spring Tulip panel, which measures 28 x 28 cm (11 x 11 in).

7 Slip-hem the bias tape down along both edges with a thread to match the tape. Work the inner edges of the curves first, then the outer edges. Remove all tacking stitches before adding a border.

Quilting

Italian Quilting

Sashiko

Trapunto

Italian Quilting

Wool or cord threaded through stitched channels forms a raised, linear design in the technique of Italian or corded quilting. It was used as a form of decoration on quilts and clothing as early as the 17th and 18th centuries, and enjoyed a revival in the 1930s and '40s. Corded quilting is more decorative than practical; it cannot be padded and this is one possible explanation of its name, since warmer bedcovers were not so necessary in the Mediterranean climate. Light coloured fabrics are most suitable for projects in Italian quilting as they show off the sculptured effect more easily. Designs can be adapted from various sources; plant forms, Celtic knots, hearts and circles, for example, could all be starting points.

1 Plan your design and make the necessary templates. Cut a piece of the top fabric allowing extra for turnings. The fabric for the back should have a loose weave so that a blunt needle can be pushed between the threads without cutting a hole in it. Muslin is suitable. Cut a piece the same size as the top and smooth them together, then tack them to prevent the layers from shifting. Mark the design on the top fabric.

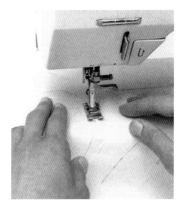

2 Stitch along the marked lines by hand or machine in double channels, a scant 0.75 cm (¼ in) apart. If sewing by hand use a running or back stitch. If sewing by machine use a medium stitch. If the design has lines which cross each other, decide which will be a continuous line and stop the intersecting lines of stitching at the point where they cross each other so the cord can be threaded through.

3 Thread a blunt needle with a big eye with a length of quilting wool and, working from the back, insert the needle into the stitched channel, pushing it between the loose weave of the backing fabric and the top fabric. Slide the needle along as far as possible, then bring it out further along the channel and pull gently to ease the wool through, leaving an end of about 0.75 cm (¼ in). Reinsert the needle through the same opening and continue, leaving a small loop at the point of exit so that the wool will lie smoothly on curves and angles. At the end of the length bring the needle out and cut off the wool leaving 0.75 cm (¼ in). If the design is circular, starting and finishing at the same point, stitch the two ends together to prevent them from disappearing into the channel.

4 Completed panel of Italian quilting using simple heart-shaped motifs.

WHOLECLOTH QUILTS

Italian or corded quilting has often featured on quilts made throughout Europe, as well as in Asia and the Middle East. The wholecloth quilt illustrated above uses Italian quilting to provide intricate decoration and relief. The designs of wholecloth quilts are characteristically inspired by everyday objects, such as feathers, shells, fans, or, as in this case, flowers and leaves. The use of the same colour thread for the quilting as the background fabric is also typical of wholecloth quilting, and contributes to its simple, traditional quality.

Sashiko

Sashiko is a form of quilting which originated in Japan as a plain running stitch to strengthen or repair fabric, either padded or unpadded. The resulting fabric was put to a variety of uses, notably in firemen's clothing (which would be drenched with water before firefighting), and in clothing and household furnishings. Decorative sashiko stitching developed during the 18th century and was used for embellishing kimonos, hangings and futon covers. Designs such as Hempweed, Wave and Chrysanthemums were inspired by nature; others were taken from family crests. The stitches are longer than a normal quilting stitch and are made in a thread which contrasts with the cloth; black on white, or white on a blue or red ground and vice versa, are popular Japanese colours. Emphasis is placed not on the size of the stitches; it is more important that they should be even and show up well.

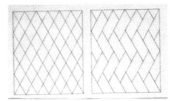

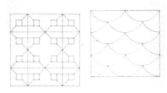

1 Start by working a square or rectangular panel of about 20 to 25 cm (8 to 10 in). A geometric design using straight lines would be a good starting project. Draw it full size on graph paper (either squared or isometric), then transfer to the fabric using dressmaker's carbon paper.

3 Begin with a knot concealed between the layers and try as far as possible to work continuous lines of stitching, which avoids breaking the thread too often.

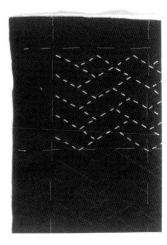

4 Try to achieve evenness in the stitches. The sashiko stitch is traditionally longer than stitches used for other quilting.

2 Assemble the layers. For preference use a flat, low-loft wadding; too much thickness will be difficult to stitch through.

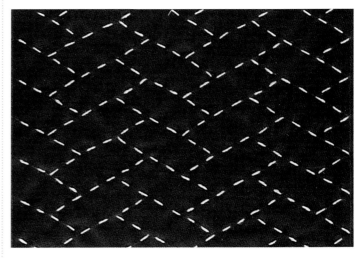

A thick thread, such as coton perle no. 3, in a colour that contrasts with the ground, will give a good definition.

Trapunto

In the technique of trapunto the top layer of the quilt or wall hanging is lined and selected areas are outlined with running stitch. Stuffing is pushed into these areas from the back to emphasise them and make them stand out more distinctly. Trapunto can be combined successfully with other forms of quilting. It is very effective with a closely quilted background, or with linear details added in Italian quilting.

It was used to decorate clothing in the 17th and 18th centuries and as a way of embellishing quilts, thus showing off the skills of the maker. Designs for trapunto should be made up of small areas which can be outlined individually. Fruit, foliage and flower shapes can all be simplified and used as a basis for trapunto designs.

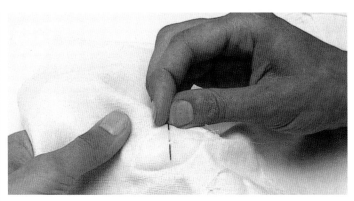

1 When you have worked out a satisfactory design, transfer it onto the top fabric. A pale coloured fabric with a slight glaze will show off the characteristics best, reflecting the light and emphasising the sculptured effect. Tack the top fabric to the backing, which should be fairly soft and loosely woven. Muslin or mull are both suitable fabrics.

3 When the area has enough padding pushed up to the stitching line, either stitch the gap with the edges just meeting, or rearrange the threads to close it. Do not pull the stitches too tightly, as this may pucker the background. If you are combining the technique with Italian quilting, work the cording at this stage as well.

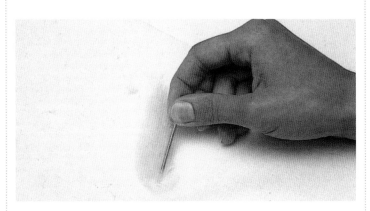

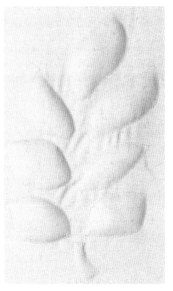

2 Stitch round each of the shapes in the design by hand or machine using a small running stitch. Finish thread ends neatly.

Make a small slit in the back of each of the shapes and gently insert wisps of stuffing, using a tool such as a knitting needle or tapestry needle with a blunt end. If the fabric has a loose enough weave you may be able to separate the threads and make an opening wide enough to insert stuffing without cutting the backing.

4 The piece can then be treated as a normal quilt top and assembled with the backing and wadding for further quilting.

Finishing

- Setting the Blocks

- Assembling the Quilt

- Binding

- Displaying Quilts

- Maintaining and Storing Quilts

Once the quilt top is complete you must decide how it is going to be quilted. Any quilt marking lines should be made before the three layers of the quilt are assembled. The simplest form of quilting is contour quilting, which follows the shape of the patchwork pieces. More complicated quilting designs can be drawn with stencils or quilting templates. Identify the centre of the quilt top and work outwards. You may need to mark guidelines on the quilt top in order to position the stencils correctly.

Quilting designs are usually made up of one or more pattern elements: motifs, which form the central focus of the design and sometimes the corner details; borders, which are linear as in running feather and cables; and infill stitches, often geometric grid-type patterns.

Quilting designs form a study in themselves, with the quilting stitches performing the dual function of holding the three layers of the quilt together as well as decorating the surface in low relief.

**JENNIE LEWIS,
IN THE POND.**
This random Log Cabin quilt has machine-stitched quilting and the border is made up of different coloured strips of fabric.

Setting the Blocks

When you have made up enough blocks to complete the quilt top, you can stitch them together in a variety of ways.

Edge to edge, straight set

Stitch them together in the same way as the blocks are made up, right sides together, matching points and taking 0.75 cm (¼ in) seam allowance. Press seams as you progress.

Alternate plain and patterned blocks

Pieced or appliquéd blocks can be alternated with plain ones. This will lessen the amount of work involved in the piecing or appliqué part of making the quilt. The plain blocks can be used as a showcase for more elaborate quilting designs.

Sashing

Stitch the blocks in rows with a strip of sashing between each one. Then stitch a long strip between the rows, making sure that the blocks line up across the strips. Sashing strips can be made of plain or harmonizing fabric, or they can have pieced details, such as connecting corner squares, set in a contrasting fabric.

Diagonal set

The quilt blocks can be set 'on point' so that squares appear as diamonds. Stitch the blocks together in diagonal, rather than straight rows. These can be all patterned or alternated with plain blocks in the same way as the straight set. Finish the end of each row with a triangle half the size of the finished block. Finish each corner with a triangle which is a quarter the size of the finished block.

Borders

If a border is required, there are various options. A plain border in harmonizing fabric will provide areas for extra quilting and serves to balance and contain the patchwork. A pieced border should complement the patchwork design. Try to relate the pieces in the border to elements in the blocks used, both by size and shape. Another option is to use several borders, perhaps alternating plain with patterned, or narrow with broader widths.

Straight-cut borders

A simple solution to the border. As the edges of the quilt top may have become stretched with handling, measure the width and length of the quilt across the centre from edge to edge; this will ensure a more accurate fit and avoid rippling edges. Cut two straight strips to the required length and width plus seam allowances, and stitch these to the sides. Now cut two more to match the width of the patchwork plus the added width of the first two border strips, and join these to the top and bottom. Press seams as you go.

Corner squares

This is a simple but effective border. Cut two strips each for the length of the sides and top of the patchwork, to the desired width of the border plus seam allowances. Cut four squares in contrasting fabric the same size as the width of the border strips. Join two strips to the sides of the patchwork. Now add the corner squares to the short sides of the remaining strips and stitch these along the top and bottom ensuring that the joins match.

2 Reverse the positions of the borders and repeat.

3 With the right sides of the borders together, line up the marked seam lines and stitch from the inner corner to the outer corner.

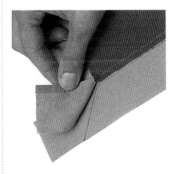

Mitred borders
1 Cut the border strips to the desired width. The length of each strip should equal the length of the side of the patchwork, plus a generous allowance for the width of the border, which will allow for the mitres. Join the borders to the patchwork right sides together, and stop the stitching at the seam allowance in each corner. Place the quilt top right side down on a flat surface and fold one border over the other. Draw a straight line from the inner corner at an angle of 45 degrees to the border.

4 Before trimming away excess fabric, open the corner seam and press it to ensure that it lies flat (above). The corner will align neatly at the front (below).

Assembling the Quilt

There are several different ways in which a quilt can be assembled, some of which are illustrated on these two pages. In each case the quilt top, wadding and backing need to be secured together. You should allow 7.5 to 10 cm (3 to 4 in) extra all round on the backing fabric and wadding. Smooth the three layers together on a flat surface and tack or pin with safety pins to prevent the layers from shifting while you work. It is important to keep the three layers taut as you sew to prevent buckling or creasing, which could impair the final result.

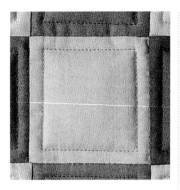

Contour quilting
Lines of stitching are done about 1 cm (⅜ in) from the seams following the outline of the patchwork shapes. Narrow masking tape can be used to mark straight lines, or you can draw them directly onto the fabric with a fabric marker.

Echo quilting
This technique, often used in Hawaiian designs (see pages 96–97), follows the lines of appliquéd shapes. Multiple lines of stitching radiate outwards to emphasize and echo the shapes.

Ditch quilting
In this case, the stitches are worked directly onto the seam lines to define the pieced or appliquéd shapes. This is a useful technique if you don't want quilting stitches to show.

Hand quilting
Hand quilting can be done on your lap, or the work can be fixed in a hoop or frame. Take a length of single quilting thread (about 45 cm [18 in]) and run it through beeswax to strengthen it and prevent knotting. Start with a knot and push the needle up from the back of the quilt, tugging until the knot pops through. The quilting stitch is a small, even running stitch through the three layers of the quilt. Work with one hand on top of the quilt and one underneath to guide the needle back and to ensure that each stitch has gone through all three layers. Protect both hands with a thimble on both the top stitching finger and the bottom guiding finger.

Random quilting
Random quilting can be worked by hand or machine. The design need not be marked as it is 'drawn' freehand as you stitch. Define the area to be quilted in this manner either by the patchwork, or by drawing a shape onto the quilt top within which to stitch. Use a freeform design which covers the area evenly and stitch by hand or machine.

Machine quilting

This can be done either with a straight sewing stitch or by dropping the feed dogs on the machine and stitching freehand.

Mark quilting lines if necessary and prepare the quilt layers as for hand quilting.

Knot quilting

The quickest way to finish a quilt is to tie knots at regular intervals to secure the three layers together, rather than stitch through them. Assemble the quilt layers as for other methods, then decide at which points on the quilt to tie the knots. The patchwork design could be used as a guide. A thicker wadding can be used to make a tied quilt, giving a puffier result. Using a strong, natural-fibre thread such as embroidery or crochet cotton, take a stitch through all three layers, leaving an end long enough to tie. Stitch again over the first stitch, bringing the needle up near the loose end. Tie in a reef knot, not too tightly as this might cause the fabric to tear. Tie at regular intervals over the quilt surface, about 10 to 15 cm (4 to 6 in) apart. The knots can be used as decorative features either by themselves or in conjunction with buttons, beads or French knots.

1 For straight-stitch machine quilting, use a walking foot if possible. This feeds the three layers of the quilt through the machine evenly. Start with three or four very small stitches, then turn the stitch length to 3. Tighten the bottom tension very slightly. Quilt in the ditch between blocks to stabilize them, then follow your desired quilting design. Try to keep the bulk of the quilt rolled up and supported on a table. Use cycle clips to keep the quilt in place.

2 Try to work out a quilting design which has as few breaks as possible and avoids turning the quilt in the machine. Place your hands round the quilting area in a triangle as it goes through the machine. Thread for machine quilting can be selected to blend or contrast with the fabrics. An invisible thread has been developed for machine quilting. When using this thread, put ordinary machine thread which matches the quilt backing in the bobbin.

3 For free machine quilting, change to the darning foot, drop the feed dogs and sew by moving the work under the needle in the desired design. If possible, avoid turning it too much in the machine. Work at a steady pace and keep the stitches a consistent size. When the feed dogs are dropped you have to control this. Pull thread ends to the back and cut them off close to the quilt surface.

Binding

When quilting is completed, the raw edges of the quilt must be neatened. This can be done in various ways.

Binding can be made on the straight grain or the bias grain. Straight binding makes a more economical use of fabric and is therefore more suitable for large quilts. Bias binding is stretchy, and is therefore good for wall hangings as it will pull in the edges slightly and so help the quilt to hang flat against the wall.

Edges turned in

Trim away the excess wadding and backing fabric so that the three layers are even. Fold the backing fabric 0.75 cm (¼ in) over the wadding and turn in the top by 0.75 cm (¼ in) to the wrong side. Slipstitch the folded edges of the top and backing together, completely enclosing the wadding.

The completed cover of the quilt should align neatly with no puckered edges or wadding visible.

Self-binding

In this method the backing fabric is folded over the front of the quilt and hemmed down to neaten the edges.

Trim the wadding even with the quilt top. Mark a line 2.5 cm (1 in) away from the edges on the backing fabric and cut along the line. This leaves the backing extending beyond the edges by 2.5 cm (1 in) all the way round.

Bring the backing over the front of the quilt with a double fold, enclosing the wadding and raw edges. Hem down on the right side of the quilt.

At the corners fold the backing so that the point touches the corner point of the quilt top and trim away excess fabric along the crease. Then fold the ends under to form a mitre (see page 105) and continue hemming the backing over the front of the quilt.

Making the binding

A double binding is easier to handle and gives a neater and stronger finish.

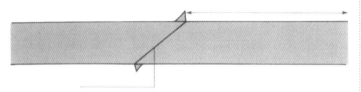

Straight binding

Cut strips on the straight grain of the fabric from selvedge to selvedge 5 to 6 cm (2 to 2½ in) wide. If it is necessary to join strips a join on an angle is less noticeable.

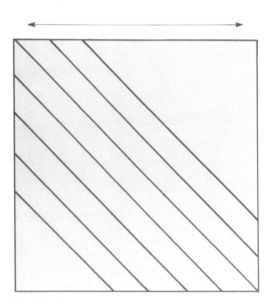

Bias binding

1 Cut the strips diagonally across a square of fabric. One square metre/yard will make approximately 16 m (17½ yds) of 5-cm (2-in) wide bias binding.

2 To join pieces place the straight grain ends right sides together and stitch, taking 0.75 cm (¼ in) of seam allowance.

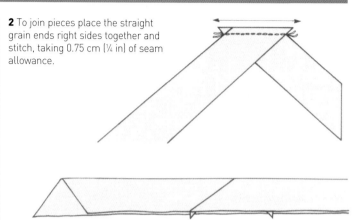

3 Press seams open, fold the binding strip in half lengthwise and press. Trim away seam allowance ends.

Whether you are using straight or bias binding, there is now one side with two raw edges and one side with a fold.

Applying binding

To apply binding, begin in the centre of one side of the quilt and place the raw edges against the edges to be bound. Stitch through both layers of the binding and through all layers of the quilt, taking 0.75 cm (¼ in) seam allowance. The folded edges of the binding can then be turned over the raw edges of the quilt and hemmed down on the back of the quilt.

Displaying Quilts

Although quilts were made originally to be displayed on the horizontal plane of a bed or table, their decorative qualities were always considered by the maker and admired by the viewer. As early as the 19th century, quilts were displayed as hangings in shows and competitions, albeit temporarily. By the 1920s quilts were becoming collectible and the combination of their visual and tactile qualities made them an appealing addition to interior decoration. Today, more quilts than ever before are being made for vertical display as wall hangings.

A newly completed quilt should be signed and dated by the maker. Embroider the relevant details directly onto the back of your quilt or onto a label which can be stitched to the back. Indelible pens with which you can write straight onto fabric are also available.

To display as a wall hanging, either sew a continuous casing along the top through which a hanging rod can be inserted, or use Velcro tape. Whichever method you use, cut the wood marginally shorter than the width of the quilt so it will be concealed when the quilt is hung. Choose a hanging position out of direct sunlight to preserve the colours in the fabrics and be aware of other atmospheric conditions which may damage a quilt; smoke and damp should be avoided. A quilt should not be hung indefinitely; it is a good idea to 'rest' textiles for a short period after six months or so.

Making a hanging sleeve

Measure the width of the quilt and cut a piece of fabric to this length and 20 to 25 cm (8 to 10 in) wide. Fold in half lengthwise with right sides together and stitch into a long tube; turn right side out. Turn a narrow hem to the inside at each end, leaving the ends open. Slip-hem the casing tube along its two long edges across the top of the quilt. A batten or rod which does not touch the back of the quilt can be inserted through the casing and suspended at each end.

For a very heavy quilt, make the casing in two sections so that the quilt can be supported in the centre by a third hanger. Turn under a narrow hem at each end of each section of casing before hemming the two tubes to the back of the quilt leaving a gap in the centre to expose the rod.

Using Velcro tape

Cut a length of 5-cm (2-in) wide Velcro slightly shorter than the width of the quilt top. Machine stitch one side of the Velcro to a length of cotton tape, then hand stitch this to the reverse side of the quilt along the top. Stitch through the backing and filler so that the quilt will be adequately supported, but make sure that no stitches show on the front of the quilt.

The other side of the Velcro is then glued to a length of wood which can be fixed in place where the quilt is to hang. To attach the quilt to it, apply even pressure so that the quilt will be adequately supported.

Maintaining and Storing Quilts

The time, skill and materials invested in the making of any quilt deserve consideration in its treatment and care. It is sensible to try and preserve it, therefore, whether its value is primarily as a part of family history or whether it is a contemporary quilt to be enjoyed both now and in the future.

If you have an old quilt which needs cleaning, remember it may be fragile and must be cleaned with this in mind. Silk and wool should always be dry-cleaned; seek a quality dry-cleaner with a good reputation; the wardrobe department of a theatre may be able to advise.

Cotton and linen could be washed if the fabrics are not too damaged. First remove loose dust by spreading the quilt on a flat surface, covering it with muslin and vacuuming it on a gentle setting. Test fabrics for dyefastness by pressing dampened white blotting paper against them. Wash the quilt by hand in the bath, agitating gently in several changes of water. Use a mild detergent; gentle ones are available for delicate fabrics. Use the shower to rinse out any remaining cleaner. Squeeze out as much excess water as possible by hand. To dry the quilt, place it flat on layers of absorbent material such as towels. Do not strain old fabrics and delicate stitching with the weight of the remaining water by hanging them.

New quilts can be machine washed on the gentle programme of the washing machine using a mild, colour-care detergent. If all fabrics have been prewashed before the quilt was made, there should be no problem with colours running.

All fabrics, whether new or old, should be protected from direct sunlight to avoid fading the colours and damaging any of the fibres.

Quilt storage

Anyone with knowledge of textile conservation will tell you that correct storage is an important factor in preserving and extending the life of all fabrics. Whether you are storing old or new quilts, the following points are applicable. Try, if possible, to store quilts flat; on a bed is the ideal place. If this is not practical, roll the quilt around a long, cardboard tube covered with acid-free tissue paper, using tissue to separate the layers as well. If folding is the only storage method possible due to shortage of space, refold every two or three months to prevent the fabrics from wearing at the creases, and pack the layers with acid-free tissue paper. Wrap quilts, whether rolled or folded, in white cotton sheeting, never polythene, and store in a dry atmosphere. Damp causes mildew which will permanently mark fabrics.

Make sure that quilts are clean before putting them into storage, as the fibres can also be damaged by dust and grime. Shake gently to remove any dust and use the vacuum cleaner as previously described if washing or dry-cleaning is not possible.

JENNY REES
FAN QUILTS
Proper maintenance will ensure colours never fade and preserve the quilt for future generations.

Themes

The versatility of quiltmaking as a means of creative expression has been increasingly recognised by needleworkers at every level of ability. To interpret or reproduce the traditional patterns gives many people the satisfaction of making something both useful and beautiful. Alternatively, the techniques involved provide a basis for experimentation, leading to uniquely individual works. Historical reasons for making quilts have always been diverse, ranging from economic necessity to the exhibition of elaborate needlework and expensive fabrics. The time and skill expended on historical quilts are apparent in the artistry of contemporary quiltmakers, illustrating the enduring attraction of this imaginative craft.

Traditional Quilts

Traditional quilt designs are those that have been passed on through generations of quiltmaker, reflecting the basic principles of quilt design. These traditions are defined by techniques, those of patchwork, appliqué and quilting being the basics from which others grew.

There are many forms within these traditions. Block quilts can be simple, as in the nine-patch square, or more elaborate, using smaller and more complicated shapes or curved seams in patterns. Medallion quilts, with a large central motif enclosed in a series of borders, test the design skills of the quiltmaker and can combine the two techniques of appliqué and patchwork. The wholecloth quilt, another traditional form, exploits the texture that close stitching through the three layers of a quilt creates, with highly intricate designs stitched on plain fabric.

Many quilt historians make the link between quiltmaking and a more diverse social history of women, drawing references from examples documented in contemporary diaries and letters. A patchwork quilt containing scraps of fabric from family clothing and household furnishings was often the only link with home for a young bride living far from her loved ones. Needlework was seen as a necessary accomplishment for all girls, and quiltmaking was often taught from an early age to develop these skills.

◀ **KATHARINE GUERRIER**
LOG CABIN, COURTHOUSE STEPS
35 x 35 cm (14 x 14 in)
The Courthouse Steps Log Cabin block is just one variation of this versatile design. Dark and light value fabrics are placed opposite each other in the block. When these are used in multiples, a design reminiscent of Chinese lanterns emerges. A narrow, stripped border contains the quilt blocks, emphasizing the linear qualities of the pattern.

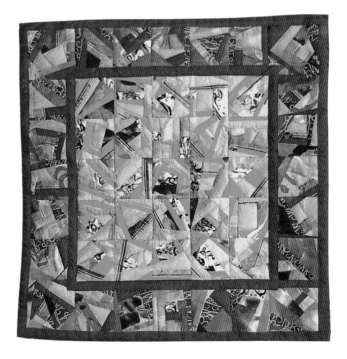

**◀ FAIRFIELD PROCESSING CORP.
GROUP QUILT**
AMERICAN HERITAGE QUILT
165 x 203 cm (65 x 80 in)
This 'American Heritage' quilt
uses a variety of techniques to
celebrate its themes. Key events
in the history of the United States
of America are presented within
a patriotic framework which uses
elements of the Stars and Stripes
to link the separate blocks. These
are made in a combination of
techniques which include
patchwork, appliqué and quilting.
Further details are added to the
quilt with embroidery.

KLARA ATALLA ▶
CHALLENGE 2
79 x 79 cm (31 x 31 in)
A machine-pieced and hand-
quilted crazy quilt which uses the
'centre piece' method. That is,
random shapes are added to a
centre piece to make the individual
blocks. The distinct colour changes
between the main part of the quilt
and the border make a pleasing
contrast between the two areas.

◀ INGRID WIELAND
DELFTER IMPRESSION
119 x 84 cm (47 x 33 in)
This appliqué basket quilt has the naive charm of much folk art. A central medallion with its flower bouquet made of many blue fabrics, some of which use three-dimensional effects, is framed by a narrow blue octagon on a cream ground. Border details of repeating flower heads and leaf swags finish the composition. The combination of cream and blue gives this quilt the delicate appeal of Delft china.

POLLY MITCHELL ▶
SOPHIE'S QUILT
188 x 188 cm (74 x 74 in)
Amish-style basket blocks in a typical range of colours form the centre of this quilt. They are surrounded by a red border with pink corner squares. Broad outer borders provide plain areas for hand-quilted running cable designs. A mix of cultures is represented in this quilt; to quote the maker, 'Sophie wanted an Amish design and was studying in China at the time, so the quilting patterns were inspired by Chinese symbols and decoration'.

SUZON DE MARCILLY ▲
L'ÉTOILE DE MARINIÈRE
241 x 241 cm (95 x 95 in)
Composed of elements from the Mariner's Compass and Broken
Star designs, this is a challenge for the ambitious quiltmaker.
The example shown here displays a sensitive choice of colours
in earth tones enlivened by flashes of yellow. The large star is
set on a cream ground and contained by a double border with
corner details reflected from the central design.

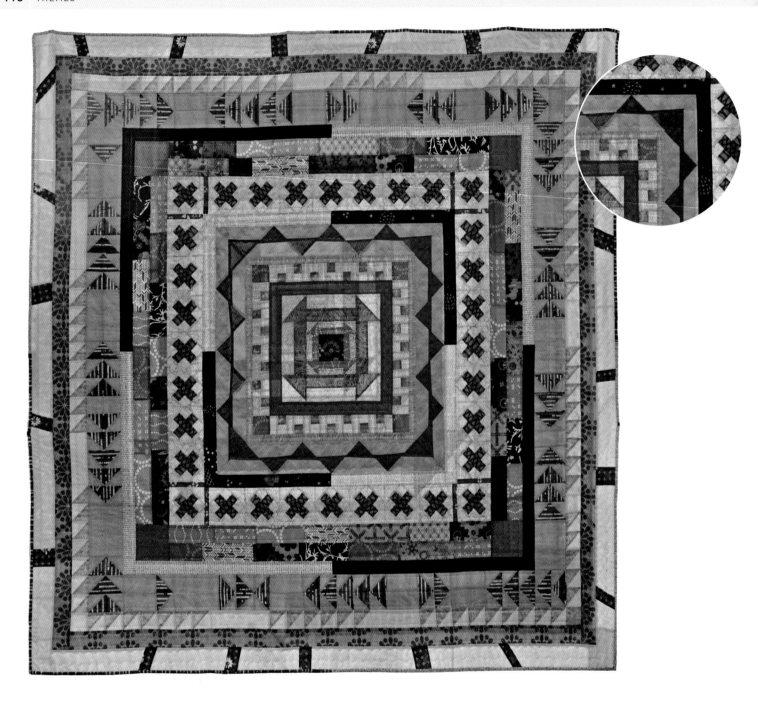

◀ **DEBBIE JESKE**
CONFECTIONERY
200 x 200 cm (80 x 80 in)
A variety of coloured and textured materials are used to produce this candy store-inspired, pick-and-mix quilt. Machine-pieced and -quilted, improvisational and traditionally pieced rows give a unique twist to this modern medallion quilt.

NANCY BRELAND ▲
FIRST LIGHT
132 x 170 cm (52 x 67 in)
An extensive collection of blue and cream fabrics are displayed in this elegant quilt. Skilful handling of colour values gives an impressionistic view of the dawn rising slowly upwards towards the stars, still shining in the night sky. Their sharp points, together with the circular secondary designs, convey a dynamic energy. The quilt was machine-pieced and hand-quilted.

MARY PONA ▲
WINDMILLS
114 x 152 cm (45 x 60 in)
This mosaic-like quilt is created using a freehand-cut curve technique, so no individual block on this quilt is exactly the same. The quilt, which uses a different patterned background for each 'windmill', uses colours that are both neutral and complementary. This piece was machine-pieced and machine-quilted.

GILL TURLEY ▶
FABRIC OF OXFAM
137 x 193 cm (54 x 76 in)
This rather striking quilt was
made entirely from recycled
shirting fabrics purchased in
charity Oxfam shops. A cross-
shaped central medallion is set
in a grid of geometric shapes in
a muted, monochromatic colour
scheme which is pleasingly
sombre. The patches were rotary
cut and machine-pieced and the
quilt is finished with a double
bias binding and tie quilting.

◄ **DEBBIE JESKE**
SNOOZE ALARM
56 x 56 cm (22 x 22 in)
Created using the Wake Up Call block by Amy Gunson, this striking quilt is matchstick quilted with multiple lines of stitching sewn really close together.

◄ **GILL TURLEY**
WILD ROSE
102 x 102 cm (40 x 40 in)
A wholecloth quilt with a centre diamond medallion containing Celtic and fan motifs with a fine, feather border. A straight filling pattern and more fans separate the outer border from the centre square, which is composed of flowing, floral scrolls (detail). The effect created by the stitching in this composition is that of a bas-relief carving.

◀ **NATALIA MANLEY**
OLIVIER'S QUILT
297 x 318 cm (117 x 125 in)
The traditional pineapple motif
(detail of back, above) is combined
with that of Birds-of-Paradise in
this Hawaiian appliqué quilt. It is
reversible, with a simplified
version of the appliqué on the
back. Completed in the traditional
style of quilting, which echoes the
central appliqué or 'Kapa Lau', this
is a fine example of the form.

◀ **MARY PONA,**
DOUBLE WEDDING RING
146 x 146 cm (57½ x 57½ in)
A fresh, modern take on the
traditional Double Wedding Ring
quilt. This striking quilt has flashes
of gold, silver and purple and is an
example of the possibilities that
can be achieved using freehand-
cut techniques. Machine-pieced
and quilted.

◀ **GILL TURLEY**
STARS OF THE NORTH
112 x 112 cm (44 x 44 in)
This quilt is a variation of the Log
Cabin block; by altering the width
of the strips between the light and
dark sides of each block, an
illusion of curved lines is achieved.
Skilfully handled colour values in a
restricted palette of greys add to
the illusion by making the dark
stars seem to float in front of the
lighter diamond shapes behind
them. The quilt was machine-
pieced and hand-quilted and
finished with a double binding.

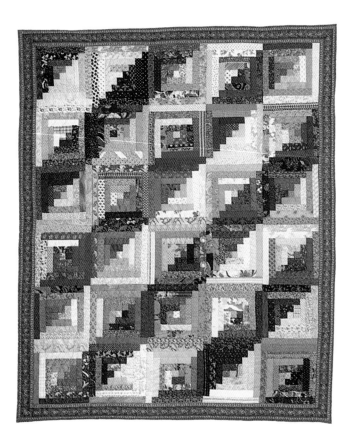

◀ **GILLIAN NEWBERRY**
CHARM QUILT
218 x 218 cm (86 x 86 in)
The Log Cabin design is an all-time favourite and ideal for making scrap quilts. This example, set in the Straight Furrow variation, is also a charm quilt, that is, no fabric is used more than once. Different scale printed fabrics enliven the quilt surface, making points of interest to hold the eye. The quilt is nicely framed with a narrow border fabric. It was machine-pieced and hand-quilted.

JENNI DOBSON ▶
WINTER'S JOY
160 x 112 cm (63 x 44 in)
Circular Japanese-inspired Marumon blocks are hand appliquéd, then scattered and hand stitched to the peach-coloured background. Most of the blocks feature some hand embroidery. The background is hand-quilted in a traditional Japanese design called 'Sayagata'. The outer border is turned to the back and hand-sewn in place.

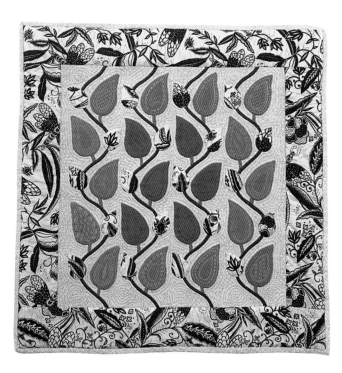

◀ **KATHLEEN E. HORNER**
PINK LEAVES
76 x 76 cm (30 x 30 in)
The pink leaves are hand
appliquéd, some being first
embellished with machine
embroidery. The stems are made
from a 2.5-cm (1-in) bias strip and
are also hand appliquéd. The
contour quilting is done 'by eye',
not marked. A narrow binding
finishes the edge.

FREDERIKE KOHLHAUSSEN ▶
SNAIL TRAIL
135 x 135 cm (53 x 53 in)
A symmetrical arrangement of
this intriguing traditional pattern,
the contrast is between coloured
and black fabrics. The effect is of
curves, but only straight seams
are used. The colouring in the
corner blocks provides a different
focus, further underlining the
illusion. The quilt was machine-
pieced and hand-quilted.

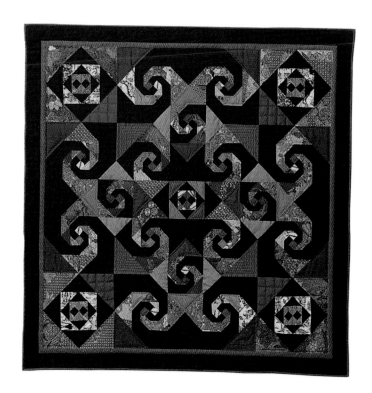

◀ JO WALTERS/
ERNESTINE DEARWENT
BUT SOFT
112 x 142 cm (44 x 56 in)
Machine-pieced 'Bowtie' blocks in
an octagonal set, many of which
feature hand-dyed fabrics, give
this quilt a luminous quality. The
regularity of the blocks is offset by
the subtle colour variations within
the fabrics. A narrow inner border
separates the blocks from the
outer border of pieced strips,
ranging through the colours
from dark to light.

◀ NANCY BRELAND
MOSAIC
191 x 147 cm (75 x 58 in)
The complex geometry of this quilt
rewards sustained study for the
many secondary designs which
become apparent. Made as 'an
experiment in using yellow', it
contains many different fabrics
organised into a coherent,
complete design. Machine-pieced
and hand-quilted.

KATHARINE GUERRIER ▶
BROKEN DISHES MINIATURE
38 x 38 cm (15 x 15 in)
Deceptively simple, this quilt
is made from a combination of
plain and pieced blocks. While
it is made up of only eight
triangles, by alternating these
with plain squares and placing
them in the diamond set with a
centre star, a more sophisticated
design emerges. The printed
fabric is Javanese batik. The
quilt was machine-pieced and
machine-quilted.

◀ KATHLEEN E. HORNER
STRIPPY QUILT – FLYING GEESE, BLUE DAISY
196 x 249 cm (77 x 98 in)
The strip-pieced quilt is a traditional form typical of the north-east of
England. This example is machine-pieced using the quick-piecing rotary-
cut method. The quilting pattern (detail above) was devised to complement
the straight lines. Large daisy shapes were drawn onto the quilt top using
a hand-made template, and the rest of the quilting designs were added
freehand using an artist's coloured pencil. The quilting was stitched by
hand in a large frame and the edges turned in and hemmed together.

ANGELIKA SÖLCH ▶
HOCHZEITS/WEDDING QUILT
150 x 220 cm (59 x 87 in)
Designed as a gift to
commemorate a wedding day,
this quilt has been made using
all cotton materials and backed
with the same red and orange
colour scheme. Made by sewing
panels of a repeated pattern
together and then using a rotary
cutter to make triangles.

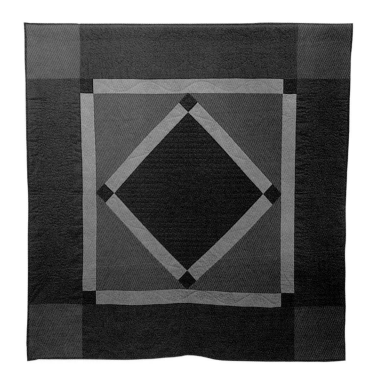

GENE BOWEN ▶
AMISH CENTRE DIAMOND
193 x 193 cm (76 x 76 in)
A traditional Amish-inspired quilt
of classic simplicity. The centre
diamond is bordered in grey with
corner squares, and set in a red
ground. Further borders add to the
overall design and provide areas
for some of the traditional quilting
motifs of the Amish: flowers, vines
and baskets.

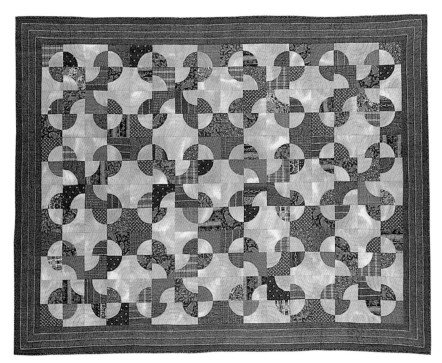

◀ JO WALTERS
'I AM A FRIEND OF BILL W.'
DRUNKARD'S PATH VARIATION
112 x 142 cm (44 x 56 in)
This simple block with a curved
seam, ideal for a scrap quilt, joins
a dark piece and a light piece
together. The blocks can then be
set in a variety of different designs
according to the direction in which
the dark/light lines are placed. In
this version the darks and lights
are reversed alternately, which
serves to produce a complex
secondary design. Machine-pieced
and hand-quilted.

Improvised Quilts

Rather than just reproducing traditional quilt patterns, some quilters draw on the same wide range of sources as artists working in other media. This is not to say that the traditions in quiltmaking are completely disregarded, but rather expanded and interpreted through more improvised quiltmaking.

Quilters have long used their chosen medium to make personal statements, exploring fresh avenues and developing new techniques. Quilts are no longer thought of as purely functional, and many quiltmakers are producing work specifically intended for display. The quilt is now accepted as a craft-based contemporary art and worthy of attention just as 'fine' art is, and subject to the same critical appraisal.

Whatever the initial source of inspiration, these quilts represent an exciting collection by artists keen to express their creative ideas and beliefs in fabric and stitching.

◀ BETHAN ASH
TRAMP ART 3
203 x 241 cm (80 x 95 in)
Strip and Seminole techniques are used in this vibrant quilt, inspired by the silk fabric. The maker says, 'I really wanted a quilt which would shout "look at me, I want to be noticed"!' More, and similar, fabrics were collected and the desired effect was achieved. Machine-pieced and machine-quilted.

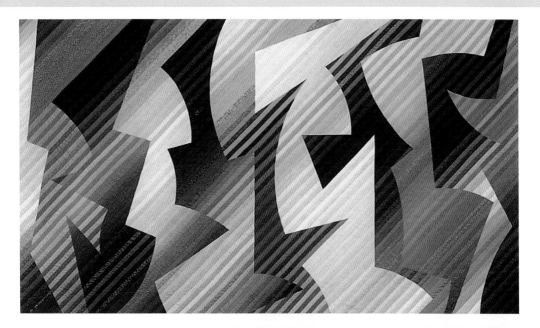

◀ MICHAEL JAMES
PROCESSIONAL
173 x 300 cm (68 x 118 in)
Michael James has a distinguished career as a quiltmaker, being one of the foremost American practitioners of the craft. In commenting on this piece, one of a group of five quilts made in 1992, he is quoted as saying, 'In Processional the intent was to reflect a series of highly formalised movements, such as those that might define a traditional Japanese dance or pantomime. Each visual gesture here is dependent on the sequences of tensions and forces that exist among the bracketing and bracketed figures'.

◀ IRENA GOOS
MEETING
102 x 130 cm (40 x 51 in)
'A fascination with space, light and movement' inspired this quilt. These concepts are expressed with a powerful three-dimensional effect created by the manipulation of colour, tonal value and shape. The quilt was machine-pieced with straight and curved seams, and machine-quilted.

◀ **NELDA WARKENTIN,**
KALEIDOSCOPE
92 x 92 cm (36 x 36 in)
This attention-grabbing quilt, with its vibrant primary and secondary colour scheme, layers many bold, single-tone acrylic-painted silks over canvas, and then stitches them together to achieve a unique kaleidoscopic effect. Machine constructed and machine quilted.

KATHARINE GUERRIER ▶
CRAZY STARS 1
152 x 152 cm (60 x 60 in)
This quilt forms part of a series in the exploration of colour values in dark, medium and light. Crazy Stars 1 is composed of dark/light diamond-shaped blocks, divided into contained crazy shapes and linked by stars which are visible because they contrast with the values in the main body of each block. Corner blocks composed of dark shapes with light 'floats' define the large diamond. The quilt is machine-pieced and machine-quilted and uses many hand block-printed and batik fabrics.

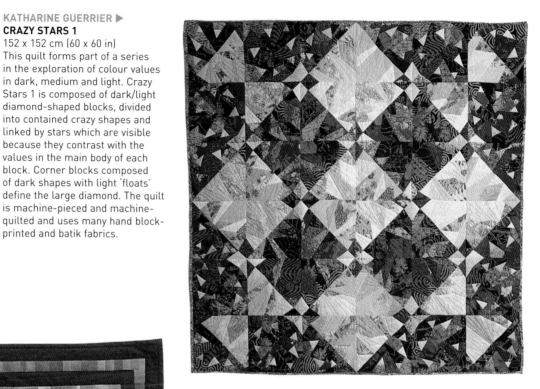

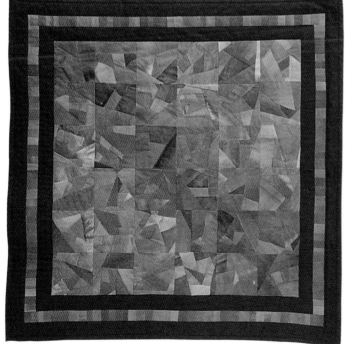

◀ **HEIDRUN RINNER**
MOSAIK
99 x 99 cm (39 x 39 in)
A desire to combine patchwork and fabric dying led to the creation of this quilt. The technique used – machine crazy patchwork – is described by the maker: 'I started with a piece of fabric in the centre and worked around clockwise as you go. I continued until a square was filled, then I placed the squares in an arrangement of my choice and set the blocks together'. Machine-pieced and hand-quilted.

▲ PAT BISHOP
SPRING WOODS
86 x 116 cm (34 x 46 in)
Inspired by the woods in northern
Wisconsin in the springtime, this
abstract quilt merges different
shades of maroon, ochre and
brown, spiked with chartreuse.
This effect has been achieved
by using commercial, hand-dyed
and repurposed textiles. The
work was machine-quilted.

◀ CAROLE PROCTOR
PICTURES IN THE FIRE
91 x 112 cm (36 x 44 in)
'An exploration of red fabrics'
was the starting point for this
quilt, made with rotary-cut
machine-pieced strips. The whole
image has an Art Deco feel to it
which is perfectly complemented
by the curved quilting lines made
both by hand and machine.

▲ IRENA GOOS
FLYING SCHOOL
112 x 114 cm (44 x 45 in)
The colours and curved shapes
in this quilt combine to convey
graceful movement in an attempt
by the maker to depict 'the flight of
a bird portrayed by the repetition
and movement of a flat element'.
The quilt was machine-pieced and
machine-quilted 'in the ditch'.

◀ GRANIA MCELLIOT
REFRACTED PATHWAY
122 x 137 cm (48 x 54 in)
Made for an exhibition of kimonos,
this opulent piece uses a
combination of fabrics. Silk, satin,
taffeta and suede provide a rich
mix of colour and texture. Crazy
shapes are machine-pieced for
both the outside and the lining.
The kimono is machine-quilted 'in
the ditch'.

KATE WELLS ▶
ANEMONE QUILT
259 x 259 cm (102 x 102 in)
The inspiration for this quilt
came from the vibrant colours
of anemones with black stamens,
their stems seen distorted
through a glass vase. It is made
using an adaptation of strip
patchwork and embellished
with machine embroidery. Other
details are hand painted with
acrylic fabric paints. The fabric
used, a shiny slipper satin, is
an ideal medium to portray the
glowing colours of the flowers.

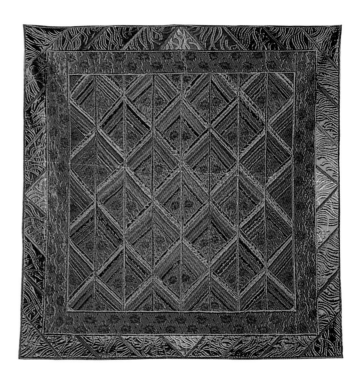

◀ RITA SCANNELL
BIRD OF PARADISE
81 x 81 cm (32 x 32 in)
An original block design made
using the Log Cabin method.
Note how the four-block panel
creates a diamond-shaped
secondary design. Spiky shapes
and hot colours in silk fabrics
are expressive of the exotic
essence of the subject. It is
machine-pieced and -quilted.

▲ KATHARINE GUERRIER
ABSTRACTIONS
71 x 71 cm (28 x 28 in)
The same machine-pieced block is repeated nine times, and although colours
and fabrics recur throughout the quilt, they are used in different positions in
every block, making each one seem very different. Blocks are also turned
about to alter their appearance even more. This is an exercise in balance –
of shape, colour and texture. Solid colours frame the blocks and the machine-
quilting zigzags across the quilt to reflect the angularity of the composition.

◄ **KATHARINE GUERRIER**
IMPROVISATION 2
63 x 61 cm (25 x 24 in)
Traditional block patterns are combined with asymmetrical Log Cabin blocks in a variety of sizes and in a mix of patterned fabrics in diverse colours. Machine-pieced and machine-quilted.

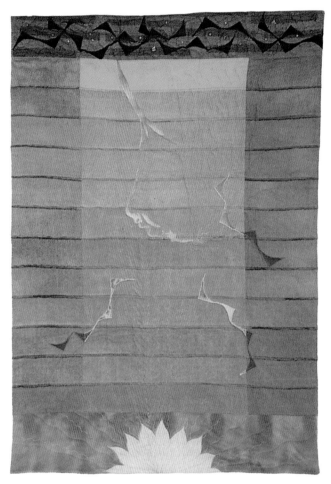

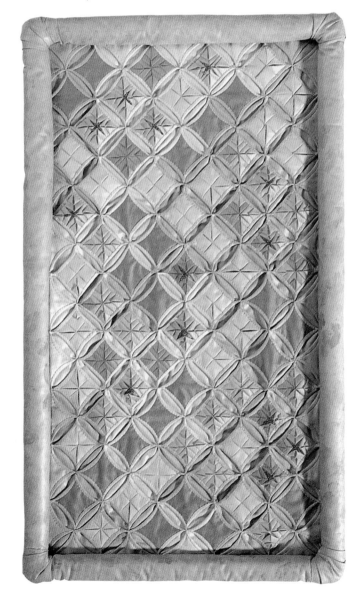

◄ **PAM DE RIVAZ**
ROSE PANEL
76 x 46 cm (30 x 18 in)
This quilt makes effective use of the Cathedral Window and Folded Star techniques. Delicate pink and green fabrics in polished cotton and silk reflect the colours of summer roses.

▲ **RITA SCANNELL**
THE DREAMER AND THE DREAM
91 x 135 cm (36 x 53 in)
In this mystical, semi-figurative image, the maker renders the weightless, floating quality of dreams. Effective use has been made of the fabrics, which include silk voile, hand dyed in close colour ranges, and organza. All stitching – the piecing, appliqué and quilting – is made by machine.

Pattern and Rhythm

In many cultures and through the ages, the principles of patternmaking, the use of repeated shapes and geometric forms, has been recognized and exploited for its ornamental aspects.

There is always something appealing about a series of repeated shapes, whether they are natural or man-made; flower petals, the formation of crystals or the spiral pattern in an ammonite, wrought-iron work, roof tiles or a contemporary city skyline. As we regard our environment, our eyes will investigate and attempt to collate these similar elements, arranging and rearranging them in a satisfactory way in which order and balance are achieved.

Decorative artists and craftsmen have drawn on this important source of inspiration to embellish their environment. Similar patterns occur in the mosaics of the Ancient Greeks and in the floor tiles of Renaissance Italy. Parallels can be drawn between the decorative elements in Early English stone tracery and those of the elaborate wrought-iron work of the Victorian era, and the geometric tile designs of the Alhambra in Spain can be compared with many quilts.

From examples in this section, it can be seen how pattern making can be a straightforward repetition of simple shapes, or more complex investigations involving colour changes within a chosen grid.

▲ GRANIA McELLIOT
FIRE OPAL KIMONO
178 x 183 cm (70 x 72 in)
A kimono-shaped wall hanging using striped and plain coloured silks. The striped fabrics are contained by a lattice of plain, bright colours symmetrically arranged. The piece was made 'as a colour exercise' and amply demostrates the evident delight the maker has in these vibrant colours. Machine-pieced and -quilted.

▲ JUDITH GAIT
ROYAL STAR BLOCK (DETAIL)
Simple shapes combined with a restricted colour scheme prove that a design need not be intricate to be effective. The controlled use of colour and the disciplined pattern demonstrate the success of such classic designs.

 JENNIE LEWIS
STAINED-GLASS WINDOW
89 x 89 cm (35 x 35 in)
A circular stained-glass window inspired this quilt made in reverse appliqué, with hand-painted silk polyester panels. It was designed to be hung in a window so that the light will shine through and illuminate the panels.

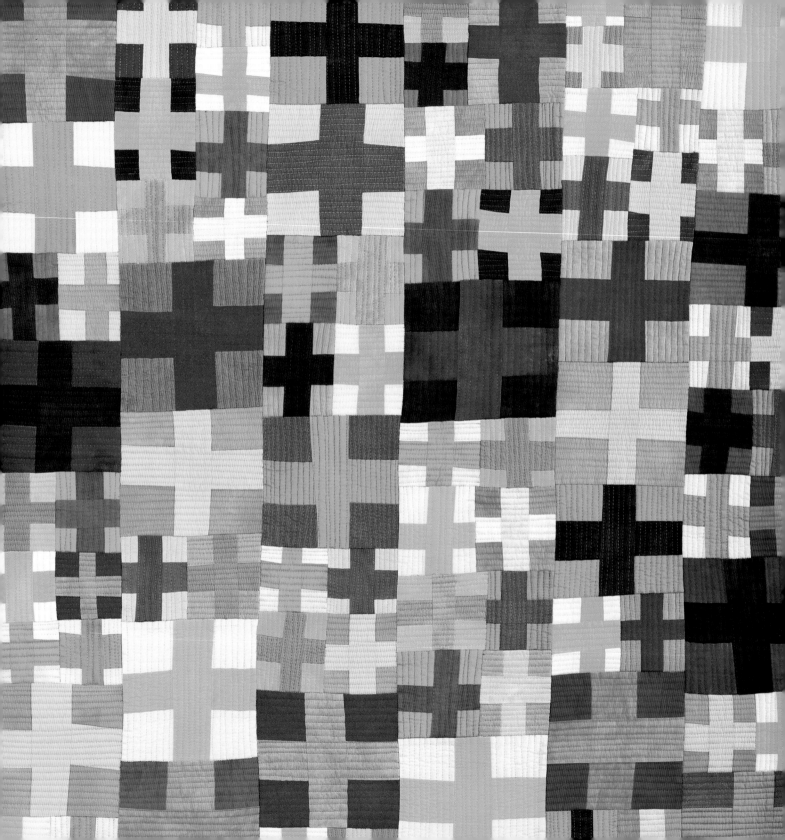

◀ **LOUISE MABBS**
ORIGAMI WINDS
76 x 76 cm (30 x 30 in)
Made for an exhibition with the
theme 'Wind', a toy pinwheel
made from folded paper provided
the idea which inspired this quilt.
Double-sided two-coloured fabric
squares are folded and sewn,
sometimes with extra padding. A
sequin secures the points of the
squares with a stitch. A border
of triangles in the same bright
colours as those used in the
centre, and contrasted with black,
completes this light-hearted piece.
Machine- and hand-stitched.

◀ **DIANE MELMS**
INTERSECTIONS
91 x 88 cm (36 x 35 in)
Bold colour and abstract design are
a characteristic of Diane's work. The
artist works from a palette of her
own hand-dyed fabrics, designing
and constructing compositions using
an improvisational method of cutting
and sewing fabric pieces together,
then finishes each piece creating a
quilt-like structure with, batting,
backing and stitching.

GRANIA McELLIOT ▶
AMETHYST
122 x 122 cm (48 x 48 in)
Another kimono-shaped hanging
from McElliot's kimono series.
This one is strip pieced using
cotton, silk and satin. Machine-
pieced and machine-quilted.

◀ **FREDERIKE KOHLHAUSSEN**
LIGHT AND SHADOW
157 x 142 cm (62 x 56 in)
A simple, regular geometric
block is changed by divisions
creating interesting variations
in the structure of the quilt.
The design was inspired by sun
shining through a window and
the fragmentation of images
thus created. Machine-pieced
and hand-quilted.

◀ **LOUISE MABBS**
**TAKING THE LIBERTY
WITH RAINBOWS**
229 x 249 cm (90 x 98 in)
A quilt seeking to explore
three- dimensional effects.
This quilt uses a wide spectrum
of colours for the framework
and a collection of geometric
Liberty prints, hence its title.
The work was machine-pieced
and hand-quilted.

INGRID WIELAND ▶
MONOGRAMME
92 x 92 cm (36 x 36 in)
With a combination of the maker's monogram and a design inspired by the artist Victor Vasarely, this quilt achieves a fine balance between the colours and shapes used. Although these are essentially simple, interest is maintained through use of the different-sized circles which serve to give the quilt a sense of movement.

ISABEL SCHNEIDER ▶
ART DECO
107 x 107 cm (42 x 42 in)
The work of artist Sonia Delaunay was the starting point for this quilt, which features a block with curved seams. This is repeated nine times, with each version made up in a different combination of clear, plain colours to break the formality of the repetition. The use of black sashing and borders separates the blocks, making each seem like a small work of art. Pieced by hand and machine- and hand-quilted.

SHELLY BURGE ▶
CHIMERA
127 x 147 cm (50 x 58 in)

An ingenious use of strip piecing is demonstrated in this contemporary quilt. It is made of equilateral triangles, with those for the star blocks first strip pieced before they are cut out. These form a broken hexagon in a field of blue triangles, and effective use is made of blue's complementary colour orange. A border of angled strips is separated from the centre of the quilt by a dark frame. The quilting design of overlapping rings was inspired by the ripples of the surface of a pond.

◀ ANN FAHL
TRIANGLES AND BEADS
155 x 119 cm (61 x 47 in)

A one-patch quilt composed of triangles, but with a complexity added by the controlled use of colour. Glowing red and turquoise areas are offset by the use of deep, rich colours which blend together in a multi-fabric composition. Bugle beads, sewn on in a diagonal geometric design, and machine-quilting emphasize the formal geometry of the quilt.

CATHERINE SCHNEIDER-MOYNOT ▲
ET LA LUMIÈRE FUT/DISAPPEARING LIGHT
106 x 106 cm (42 x 42 in)
This interpretation of the theme 'Disappearing Light' uses a complex repetition of controlled crazy blocks. These interact together to form a fragmented whole. The expert handling of colour across the surface of the quilt adds much to the impression. It is machine-pieced and hand-quilted using hand-dyed silk.

◄ GRANIA MCELLIOT
LOG CABIN QUILT
264 x 264 cm (104 x 104 in)
The Log Cabin quilt is an all-time favourite and this is a fine interpretation of the design. The blocks, set 'on point', are made in a limited palette of blues, pinks and greys in varying values, which clearly illustrate the versatility of this traditional block. Machine-pieced and -quilted.

◀ KATHARINE GUERRIER
**PINEAPPLE LOG
CABIN MINIATURE**
33 x 28 cm (13 x 11 in)
The strong contrast between
dark and light emphasizes
secondary designs when the
blocks are placed together.
Machine-pieced and -quilted.

◀ KATHARINE GUERRIER
INDIANA PUZZLE MINIATURE
38 x 38 cm (15 x 15 in)
Positive and negative interlocking shapes are created as these simple
blocks, composed only of squares and triangles, are put together. The
secret is in the placement of dark and light values within the block. A
simple stripped border is separated from the centre of the quilt by a
narrow, dark band.

Texture

When asked why they prefer the medium of fabric and stitching over others, many quilt artists say that the texture of the fabric and stitching gives a unique quality to the quilts; a tactile surface unlike that in any other media. This, combined with the visual appeal of the surface pattern on a quilt, allows the maker another dimension to explore when working with fabrics.

A textured surface can be achieved in a variety of ways. Reflective and matt-textured fabrics can be juxtaposed to contrast their individual qualities. Surface stitchering may also be harnessed to enhance the qualities inherent in the fabrics. The clever manipulation of different textures can produce the illusion of solidity or movement within the quilt.

Close quilting was originally done to prevent the raw wool or cotton filler in the quilt from bunching together at one end, but its potential as an added textural feature was realized and exploited in the elaborately stitched designs on old quilts. Other ways of achieving special effects with fabric, which can be incorporated into quilts, are outlined in the pages on techniques: experimentation may lead on to invention of your own methods. When you study these quilts, you will be aware that the discipline of traditional forms can be combined with innovative ways of using and creating texture in the fabrics. Try using these ideas for your own approach to creative expression.

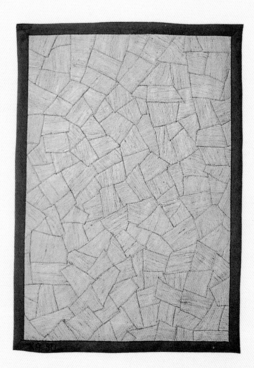

◀ KLARA ATALLA
SPLITTER/SPLINTER
56 x 78 cm (22 x 30 in)
Randomly shaped pieces of hand-woven silk have been applied to a foundation with machine satin stitch. The network of fine seams combined with the directional weave of the fabric create an interesting surface texture contained by the dark border.

RITA BALL ▶
CORNWALL, MY COUNTRY
76 x 127 cm (30 x 50 in)
A composition of squares in
delicate pastels evokes the hazy
colours of summer. To achieve
the subtle gradations, the fabrics
are all hand-dyed and the quilt
is machine-pieced. The quilting
designs, worked by hand, include
contours, shells and curves which
enhance the overall effect.

▲ GILL TURLEY
SEA AND STRATA
130 x 71 cm (51 x 28 in)
An adaptation of the Log Cabin and strip-piecing techniques are used in this impressionistic view of the seabed. The rock-like texture of the fawn fabric and its directional use blend well with the range of greys used in the upper part of the quilt. The dark outer border contains and serves to formalize the image.

MARY FOGG ▶
FABRIC ROLL
127 x 137 cm (50 x 54 in)
Strips of cotton and silk cleverly graded and stitched into this three-dimensional image complement the basic material in use. Differences in the scale of the prints used serve to emphasize the solid-looking aspect of the quilt.

DEBBIE JESKE ▶
SIZZLING
86 x 116 cm (34 x 46 in)
Fellow designer Alexander Ledgerwood inspired the block, and the quilt goes under the unofficial title of 'the bacon quilt'. Quilted using horizontal serpentine stitch to 'replicate the wave of a good bacon', this beautiful textural piece uses cottons and linen fabrics.

▲ DEBBIE JESKE
SCRAP LEATHER
43 x 43 cm (17 x 17 in)
Inspired by Season Evans and
the Mighty Lucky Quilting Club,
this densely quilted piece was
a response to a quilt challenge
built around a minimalist theme.
Using bronze brown shot cotton
as the focus fabric, the different
pieces fit together like a puzzle.
The surprise element is the
unquilted leather scrap.

◄ HELENE KNOTT
MACHINE-QUILTING AS ART
32 x 32 cm (12½ x 12½ in)
Helene's wholecloth miniature
quilt with her own leaf and tree-
patterned design demonstrates
the diverse art of quilting.

▲ LOUISE MABBS
AFRICAN KING VIOLET
152 x 249 cm (60 x 98 in)
The simplicity of each block combining
plain and patterned fabrics is an ideal
showcase for these African and
Javanese batiks. Machine-piecing with
some appliqué is combined with hand-
quilting. The quilt is finished with a
narrow patterned binding.

◄ KATHLEEN E. HORNER
NIGHT AND DAY
170 x 241 cm (67 x 95 in)
Effective use is made of graded colours and values in this geometric machine-pieced interpretation of the 'Night and Day' theme. A touch of realism is added by the appliquéd sun and moon and the hand-quilted sun rays. More hand quilting is used on the border. The centre panel is tie quilted.

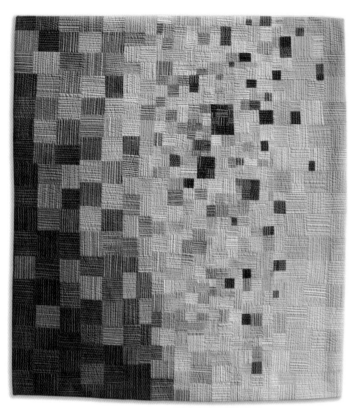

◀ DIANE MELMS
GLIMMER
91 x 81 cm (36 x 32 in)
The pixilated effect of this quilt has been achieved by the artist's keen eye for colour. The hand-dyed fabrics are painted using textile paint that helps to make the spots of red pop out from the quilt. This piece has been machine-pieced and -quilted.

LEESA ZARINELLI GAWLIK ▶
TOGETHER/SEPARATE
58 x 33 cm (23 x 13 in)
This intriguing piece is created using the heat-set shibori method and hand stitching. The fabrics are dyed with plant materials and then painted using natural dye sticks. By combining Japanese and Laotian silks, repurposed kimono linings, muslin and wool canvas, the artist has created a beautiful piece. The fabrics are loosely stitched together by hand and then machine-appliquéd and -stitched following assembly.

◀ FREDERIKE KOHLHAUSSEN
GEWACHSE
96 x 154 cm (38 x 61 in)
Large and small-scale prints are combined with plain fabrics in a range of vibrant colours. These work with the regularity of the pattern on the quilt to create a coherent surface. Attention is at first focused on the large prints, but the eye is kept moving to identify regular sequences of shape and colour. The whole design is contained by a double border and a narrow binding.

◄ CAROLE HOLLAND
INDIGO QUILT
244 x 152 cm (96 x 60 in)
The simple composition of this
quilt is all that is needed to show
off the various decorative indigo-
dyeing methods used on the
fabrics. The quilt is strip pieced
and quilted by hand with
sashiko designs.

Pictorial Quilts

Stitched pictures appear in many cultures, and the idea of using fabric and thread to make images is found throughout the world. Whether naturalistic or heavily stylised, they are a special way to capture people, places and other subjects.

There is a rich history of pictorial quilts. Banners and religious vestments were decorated with appliqué in medieval Europe, and in Nigeria large pictorial wall hangings are still made to record and celebrate events in a deceased person's life. Maori tribes of New Zealand, and North American Indians, traditionally decorate their clothing with pictures and symbols, and in Japan gold and silk are worked into elaborate appliqué panels.

The art involved in selecting the right fabric, composing the picture and stitching all the elements together is illustrated by the quilts in this section. They display a range of approaches to fabric picture making and exhibit a variety of techniques.

◀ JENNIE LEWIS
THROUGH THE ARCHED WINDOW
74 x 104 cm (29 x 41 in)
Many different techniques are used in this view into a country garden, including English paper piecing, appliqué, machine and hand embroidery, together with hand-painted and -dyed fabric. The materials are also diverse: silk, net, organdie and cotton among them. This multiplicity of techniques and materials works together to create a pleasing image which is effectively contained by the padded frame.

PAT BISHOP ▶
GAWKING CRANES
104 x 99 cm (41 x 39 in)
This quilt was inspired by the artist's visits to her parents' house, where she photographed a family of cranes scavenging for food. The detailed subjects have a contrasting vertical placement, defined shape and expressive life-like quality that invite the viewer to look at the finer details. Pat's style is to blend many different colours and tones of fabric together as if using paint. Machine-quilted.

▲ ANN FAHL
GARDEN WALL
119 x 102 cm (47 x 40 in)
Personal observation of a favourite
place inspired this quilt. The red
brick wall is recreated in fabrics
collected to reflect its colour.

◄ SHEILA DALGLEISH
WILD GERANIUMS AT ASBYRGI
15 x 30 cm (6 x 12 in)
A selection of photographed
leaves was printed out and
transferred onto a light green
fabric to create the surface
design of this beautiful nature-
inspired quilt. The leaves are
cut out and then backed with
fabric adhesive to attach them
loosely to the darker background
fabric. The machine stitching
adds the extra detail of veins to
the leaves.

FAIRFIELD PROCESSING CORP.
GROUP QUILT ►
ONCE UPON A NURSERY RHYME
165 x 165 cm (65 x 65 in)
There is plenty of visual interest in
each one of the blocks in this lively
quilt, which celebrates the nursery
rhyme theme. Appliqué techniques
are used in the blocks, which are
separated by sashing strips.

▲ NATALIA MANLEY
THE FABRIC OF LIFE IS BURNING
137 x 152 cm (54 x 60 in)
A quilt with a powerful message. In the maker's own words, 'This quilt was inspired by the appalling waste of our Earth's resources. The back of the quilt is hand painted in shades of black and grey to represent the burned-out forest'. Machine techniques include appliqué, quilting and embroidery on mixed fabrics, which include silk, cotton, satin and polyester.

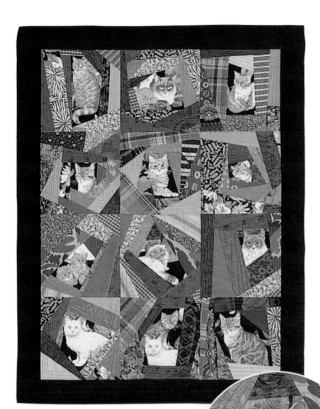

▼ ANN FAHL
FLAMINGO GARDEN
168 x 211 cm (66 x 83 in)
This elegant composition depicts flamingos in a fenced garden. Various techniques are used. The background is made of 'freeform' patchwork, a term coined by the maker to describe her particular development of strip patchwork. A lightweight fabric forms the foundation. On top, strips are sewn in a variety of ways to achieve interesting effects. The birds are machine appliquéd and the piece is embellished with beads and closely quilted by machine.

▲ KATHARINE GUERRIER
CAT CRAZY
91 x 74 cm (36 x 29 in)
A novelty fabric printed all over with cats was the starting point for this quilt. Each block has a cut-out cat in the centre and crazy shapes are added in rotation, stitched down onto a foundation using machine crazy patchwork. Blocks are joined edge to edge and the quilt has a black border finished with pieced straight binding. It is machine-quilted with different-coloured thread in each block.

MARYTE COLLARD ▲
CROCUSES IN THE SNOW
83 x 71 cm (33 x 28 in)
A flower breaking the surface of a cold and snowy landscape to catch a ray of sunshine was the inspiration behind this piece. The soft colour palette of blues, purples, greens and aquamarines was achieved by combining hand-dyed and commercial fabrics. Maryte uses curved piecing to add a natural quality to the crocus petals and stems. Machine-quilted.

INGRID WIELAND ▲
I. W. IN NEW YORK
274 x 147 cm (108 x 58 in)
In a pieced view of the New York skyline, the large self-portrait is seen as a reflection in the side of one of the buildings. The restricted colour scheme of blues, greys and black emphasizes the essential quality of the built environment.

◄ **INGRID WIELAND**
DIE HEILIGE FAMILIE
81 x 58 cm (32 x 23 in)
This portrayal of the Nativity, made in a form of reverse appliqué, has a naive charm. The simplicity of the shapes and figures in the picture and the clear colours retell this powerful story.

◀ IRENE MCWILLIAM
BUTTERFLIES
48 x 56 cm (19 x 22 in)
An abundance of butterflies
flutters over luxuriant flowers in
this fantasy garden. The flower
bed is made from a collage of
tiny, brightly coloured pieces of
fabric freely machine-stitched to
the background. This provides a
backdrop for the butterflies,
themselves made from scraps
of vibrant silks, cottons and
polycottons and machine-
appliquéd down. Further details
are added with machine-
embroidery. The edges are
neatened and finished with piping.

ANN FAHL ▶
WINONA WINTER
107 x 99 cm (42 x 39 in)
An evocative quilt which makes
use of a clever combination of
techniques. The background is
made of pieced triangles with
overlays of sheer white voile.
Icy white leaves are machine-
appliquéd, as are the blue metallic
willow leaves. Hand-beading with
bugle beads adds further to the
detail, and the piece is machine-
quilted in jagged 'icy' quilting.

◄ **LOUISE BELL**
JUNGLE
152 x 152 cm (60 x 60 in)
A cat's jungle fantasy is gloriously depicted in this quilt. The shapes were freely drawn and cut straight from the fabrics with no preliminary sketches. The picture panel was built up and stitched in progression using machine satin stitch. The whole quilt has a layer of wadding but extra padding was added to some of the animals to give them a higher profile. Final details like the veins on the leaves and the silver cobweb were added to the picture with surface embroidery, by hand and machine. The patchwork border in multicoloured Sawtooth strips with Bear's Paw corners is an appropriate finishing touch.

LOUISE BELL ▶
QUEBEC SCENE
236 x 211 cm (93 x 83 in)
An exhibition brief 'Quebec and Indian art' sparked off the many childhood memories which inspired this quilt. The maker, a native of Quebec, depicts the lake where she grew up, and has surrounded the picture with patchwork borders using relevant block designs, including Sawtooth, Fir Trees, Flying Geese, Seminole, Bear's Paw, Log Cabin and Maple Leaf designs. The piece is machine-appliquéd and machine-pieced. Surface stitching is used to add final details to the picture, and the whole is machine-quilted.

◄ ANN FAHL
DESERT PALLADIAN
102 x 152 cm (40 x 60 in)
In Desert Palladian, strip piecing, cut and stitched together again, gives a painterly effect to the desert landscape in the background. The hand-appliquéd and beaded cactus flowers in the foreground (detail above) seem to emphasize the effect of distance created by the small pieces and flowing lines. Machine-quilting gives further textural detail.

MAGDA IMREGH ▲
FLOWER VALLEY
41 x 61 cm (16 x 24 in)
A picturesque valley carpeted with
flowers in central Norway provided
the inspiration for this quilt. A
combination of different fabrics
with various surfaces – cotton,
silk, velvet and sateen – makes an
interestingly textured landscape.
The shapes are machine-appliquéd
and details are added with hand
embroidery and hand-quilting.

MAGDA IMREGH ▲
WINTER PLEASURES
23 x 30 cm (9 x 12 in)
The character in a child's story is
the starting point for this miniature
quilt. It is made with cotton, silk
and velvet, with some hand
painting on the cabin. The fabrics
are machine-appliquéd, hand-
embroidered and hand-quilted
to create the dramatic snowscape.

Index

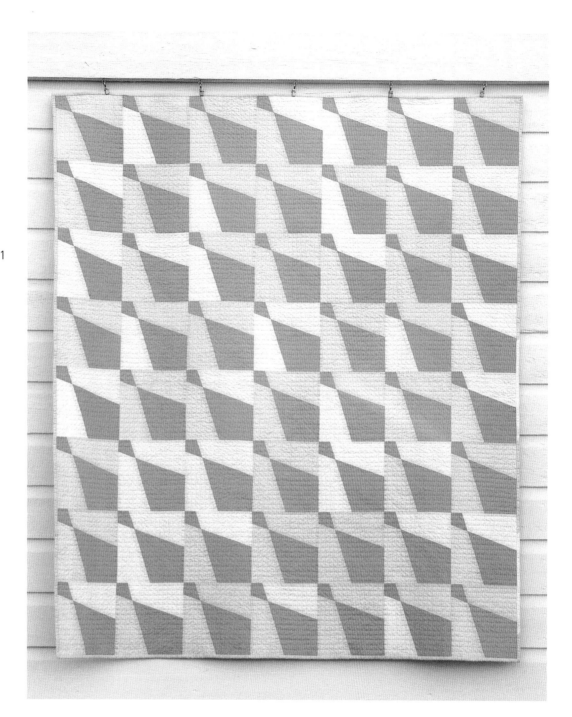

HABERDASHERY
AMY FRIEND

Credits

Quarto would like to thank the following artists for supplying images for inclusion in this book:

Ash, Bethan, p.130
Atalla, Klara, pp.115b, 150
Ball, Rita, p.151
Bell, Louise, p.169t/b
Bishop, Pat, www.patbishop.info, pp.5, 134, 161
Bowen, Gene, p.129t
Breland, Nancy, pp.23, 119l, 126b
Burge, Shelly, p.146t
Collard, Maryte, www.marytequilts.eu, p.166
Dalgleish, Sheila, www.sdalgleish.co.uk, p.162l
De Marcilly, Suzon, p.117
De Rivaz, Pam, p.139l
Debbie, Jeske, pp.6, 121t, 155tl
dimbar76, Shutterstock.com, pp.18, 112
Dobson, Jenni, p.124b
Fahl, Ann, pp.146, 146r, 165br, 168b, 170
Fairfeild Processing Corp., pp.16, 115t, 147
Fogg, Mary, p.152b
Friend, Amy, www.duringquiettime.com, p.175
Gait, Judith, p.141r
Gawlik, Leesa Zarinelli, p.157b
Goos, Irena, pp.131b, 135tr
Guerrier, Katherine, pp.84, 114, 127t, 133t, 137, 138, 149t/b, 165l
Holland, Carole, p.159
Horner, Kathleen. E, pp.125t, 127b, 156
Imregh, Magda, p.171l/r
James, Michael, p.131t
Jeske, Debbie, aquilterstable.blogspot.co.uk, pp.118, 153
Knot, Josephine, p.25
Knott, Helene, www.heleneknott.com, p.154
Kohlhaussen, Frederike, pp.125b, 144t, 158
Lewis, Jennie, pp.104, 141l, 160
Mabbs, Louise, pp.143t, 144b, 155br
Manley, Natalia, pp.123t, 164
McElliot, Grania, pp.135b, 140, 143b, 148
McWilliam, Irene, p.168t

Melms, Diane, www.dianemelms.com, pp.4, 142, 157t
Mitchell, Polly, p.116b
Newberry,Gillian, p.124t
Pona, Mary, www.funeasydesigned.com, pp.119r, 122
Proctor, Carole, p.135tl
Ramsey, Daphney, p.66
Rees, Jenny, p.111
Rinner, Heidrun, p.133b
Scannell, Rita, pp.136b, 139r
Schneider-Moynot, Catherine, p.147
Schneider, Isabel, p.145b
Sölch, Angelika,www.flickr.com/photos/quiltmakergeli/, p.128,
Tuck, Ann, p.93b
Turley, Gill, pp.120, 121b, 123b, 152t
Walters, Jo & Dearwent, Ernestine, p.126t
Walters, Jo, p.129b
Warkentin, Nelda, www.neldawarkentin.com, p.132
Wells, Kate, p.136t
Wieland, Ingrid, pp.116t, 145t, p.165t/b